Game of Thrones and the Theories of International Relations

Politics, Literature, and Film

Series Editor: Lee Trepanier, Saginaw Valley State University

The Politics, Literature Film series is an interdisciplinary examination of the intersection of politics with literature and/or film. The series is receptive to works that use a variety of methodological approaches, focus on any period from antiquity to the present, and situate their analysis in national, comparative, or global contexts. Politics, Literature, and Film seeks to be truly interdisciplinary by including authors from all the social sciences and humanities, such as political science, sociology, psychology, literature, philosophy, history, religious studies, and law. The series is open to both American and non-American literature and film. By putting forth bold and innovative ideas that appeal to a broad range of interests, the series aims to enrich our conversations about literature, film, and their relationship to politics.

Advisory Board

Recent Titles

The Final Frontier: International Relations and Politics through Star Trek and Star Wars, by Joel R. Campbell and Gigi Gokcek
Flannery O'Connor and the Perils of Governing by Tenderness, by Jerome C. Foss
The Politics of Twin Peaks, edited by Amanda DiPaolo and James Clark Gillies
AIDS-Trauma and Politics: American Literature and the Search for a Witness, by Aimee Pozorski
Baudelaire Contra Benjamin: A Critique of Politicized Aesthetics and Cultural Marxism, by Beibei Guan and Wayne Cristaudo
Updike and Politics: New Considerations, edited by Matthew Shipe and Scott Dill
Lights, Camera, Execution!: Cinematic Portrayals of Capital Punishment, by Helen J. Knowles, Bruce E. Altschuler, and Jaclyn Schildkraut
Possibility's Parents: Stories at the End of Liberalism, by Margaret Seyford Hrezo and Nicolas Pappas
Game of Thrones and the Theories of International Relations, by Laura D. Young and Ñusta Carranza Ko

Game of Thrones and the Theories of International Relations

Laura D. Young and Ñusta Carranza Ko

LEXINGTON BOOKS
Lanham • Boulder • New York • London

Published by Lexington Books
An imprint of The Rowman & Littlefield Publishing Group, Inc.
4501 Forbes Boulevard, Suite 200, Lanham, Maryland 20706
www.rowman.com

6 Tinworth Street, London SE11 5AL

British Library Cataloguing in Publication Information Available

Library of Congress Cataloging-in-Publication Data Available

ISBN 978-1-4985-6987-3 (cloth : alk. paper)
ISBN 978-1-4985-6988-0 (electronic)
ISBN 978-1-4985-6989-7 (pbk. : alk. paper)

∞™ The paper used in this publication meets the minimum requirements of American National Standard for Information Sciences Permanence of Paper for Printed Library Materials, ANSI/NISO Z39.48-1992.

Contents

Acknowledgments

This book has developed out of a series of meetings, conversations, workshops, lectures, and papers that we worked on throughout our doctoral degree at Purdue University. We are grateful for the mentorship in pedagogy we received from faculty at Purdue and the Center for Instructional Excellence, and the feedback from students who inspired us to advance further in our scholarship on teaching and learning. It is for the students that we wrote this book and it is to them that we owe our greatest thanks.

During the months we worked on this thematic focus—even before we thought of writing a book—we were given the chance to explore and present ideas related to this manuscript, which in one form or another, have now become a part of the book. We thank the discussants, chairs, and audience members who provided us with feedback at American Political Science Association and International Studies Association conferences. In addition to the comments we received at professional association meetings, a number of individuals took the time to provide us with more input and direction for our work in progress. They include Michael Perrin and Lee Trepanier. We are particularly grateful for the helpful review from Mark Sachleben and the support from Joseph C. Parry and Alison Keefner, the editors at Lexington Books.

Others who contributed in various ways to this book include Daniel Aldrich, Matthias Kaelberer, Ann M. Clark, Harry Targ, Rosalee Clawson, Patricia Boling, Marc Tilton, James M. McCann, Robert Alexander, Marie-Christine Doran, Marc Lanteigne, and Clifford Bob.

Our thankfulness to our families is greatest. We thank our children Roxanne and Marie, for collaborating with us through our writing process by napping, sleeping-well, and keeping us happy. We also thank our parents, Frank and Martha Young, and Hye Sun Ko and Francisco Carranza, and siblings Gwyn Y. Rowland and Ayra Carranza Ko who have continued to believe in our work in pedagogy and political science.

Most importantly, we thank our spouses, Giovanni Castro and Fernando Zago, for dealing with our stress, keeping us focused on the project, and rewatching the televised series of *Game of Thrones* with us on multiple occasions. We dedicate this book to them, our families, and our students, with love and respect.

Introduction

Game of Thrones Season 7, Episode 7 closes with a horrifying scene of White Walkers crossing into the North from the now crumbled wall that once stood as a fortress to protect Westeros from the Wildlings. Meanwhile, consumed with her quest for power, Cersei Lannister sits alone upon her throne as her brother Jaime rides off to join Daenerys and Jon Snow in their growing alliance to fight the inevitable war that is to come with the White Walkers. The alliance is a surprising one since Jon Snow holds the title of King of the North to which Daenerys claims as rightfully hers. Despite these differences, though, the two have banded together. Jaime's allegiance is even more surprising considering his devotion to Cersei and prior behavior would suggest the alliance with Jon Snow and/or Daenerys would not be possible under any circumstance since both challenge Cersei's right to the Iron Throne.

All the events culminate in Season 8 with the new alliance defeating the White Walkers in an epic battle. Once the foe upon which the alliance is formed is defeated, Daenerys sets her sights back to her original goal to be ruler of the Iron Throne. Cersei, certain of her victory, especially considering the losses suffered by her enemies, stands ready to face Daenerys. Before it is all over, King's Landing is completely devastated, Cersei is dead, as, too, is Daenerys (and a whole lot of others), and Jon Snow banished himself to the Wall as punishment for his deeds.

How did it come to this? When the HBO series *Game of Thrones* started, the Seven Kingdoms was ruled by King Robert Baratheon. Though the rise of Daenerys to power within the Dothraki Kingdom posed some threat to King Robert, before this, for the most part, Westeros was peaceful. Over the course of the series, though, King Robert is assassinated, as is his successor. The Seven Kingdoms broke away with regions, like the North, proclaiming their sovereignty and appointing their own king. Dorne, the Vayle, and High Garden withdrew their allegiance, as did King Robert's brother Stannis who sought to claim the Iron Throne as his own.

Throughout the series, the Seven Kingdoms continues to fall into chaos as wars break out among the different regions. Challengers from the continent of Essos and other areas like the Iron Islands seek power so they, too, can stake a claim to their own kingdom. It is only because of the growing threat of the White Walkers that Jon Snow can consolidate power over the North. It is this same threat that convinces Daenerys to align herself with Jon Snow. Unfortunately, once the threat is gone, so, too, are the allegiances that were once pledged.

The series is not unlike the events that have unfolded throughout history in international relations. Wars, the quest for power, the clash of cultures, forged alliances, and broken ones, too, are all a theme that the series has in common with the real world. George R. R. Martin is said to have drawn from historical events, like the War of the Roses (1455–1485), when writing his books. In fact, Martin is quoted as saying his model for the book "was the four-volume history of the Plantagenets that Thomas B. Costain wrote in the 50s" (Flood 2018, para. 4). So, it is no wonder events in the series so closely mirror those that occurred in the real world at one time. This makes *Game of Thrones* the perfect backdrop for explaining international relations.

WHAT IS THE STUDY OF INTERNATIONAL RELATIONS?

To define international relations as the study of state behavior in the international system is an overly simple way of thinking about the definition. The actual field of international relations is much more complex than the definition implies. As the world becomes more interconnected, so, too, does the study of international relations. In fact, international relations is very interdisciplinary in nature and seeks to explain a broad range of issues in international society and affairs. Political psychologists, for example, attempt to understand individual political behavior and decision-making to better explain state behavior. Political economists, on the other hand, are more concerned with the relationship between production, trade, and the distribution of wealth and how these variables impact international policy, politics, and society. Others focus on human rights, economic development, the environment, globalization, global ethics, and security issues like terrorism, resource scarcity, and ethnic conflict, though none of these issues are mutually exclusive and, rather, overlap in many ways.

A primary focus of international relations is understanding the origins of war and the ability of states to cooperate. As far back as the Greek historian Thucydides (c. 460–395 B.C.), scholars have concerned themselves with the exercise of power by states within the global system and how these power arrangements facilitate or hinder cooperation. Power, in fact, is a prime focus of the field. Theorists devote significant time to defining power, understanding the nature of power, determining how one goes about getting power, and figuring out how much power is enough power. Scholars also examine the affect power has on state behavior and the international system and hypothesize how states can overcome their need for power to promote a more cooperate global environment.

International relations is not just focused on power, though. The field is also concerned with the changing nature of state and non-state actors and the impact these new actors have on state behavior. Increased non-governmental organization (NGO) activity in a state, for example, helps promote more democratic norms and respect for the rule of law and, thus, facilitates a more cooperative environment. Terror groups, on the other hand, pose a new threat to state sovereignty and the security of states, domestically and internationally. As a result, these new groups can prompt an increase in international conflict. Understanding these new actors and the role they play in the international system gives scholars a clearer picture of the conditions states face, and why some are better able to avoid conflict compared to others.

Because the world is so complex, and many different factors can impact the behavior of states, it is necessary to find ways to simplify the world in which we live. Therefore, international relations relies on a set of theories and different levels of analysis to help understand and make predictions about state behavior. These theories act as roadmaps which allow one to view the world through a more simplified lens; without them, our explanatory power would be limited. For example, if you want to explain why the different conflicts took place in *Game of Thrones*, you could spend hours retelling the various events, weaving in and out of a myriad of details. Or, you could examine it from a few assumptions, like the need for power, or the lack of the rule of law and international institutions, or a disregard for basic human rights, or even by examining the individual characteristics of each leader. Using this approach makes it easier to understand why the events occurred.

International relations is an increasingly relevant field of study. As the world continues to grow and become more interconnected, the need to understand state behavior and the interactions that take place among states becomes even more important. International relations provides an interdisciplinary approach with a range of foci all of which aim to do just that. The theories it presents can help even the novice understand the complex world in which we all live.

GAME OF THRONES AND THEORIES OF INTERNATIONAL RELATIONS

When watching the series *Game of Thrones,* it is hard not to see similarities between events in the show and things that occur in the real world. Unlikely alliances defined both WWI (1914–1918) and WWII (1939–1945) (e.g., Russia and China joined forces with the United States and Great Britain to fight Germany; Italy switched sides from one war to the next, etc.). The struggle for power has defined international relations since at least the time of the Peloponnesian War (431–404 BCE), and we see it happen time and time again culminating in several major wars through-out history. The struggle for power also defines the relationships in the series *Game of Thrones*. From Robert to Stannis, Cersei to Daenerys, Marjorie to Lord Baelish, and the Greyjoys to the Boltons, just to name a few, all seek power. As a result, wars are a common theme in the series just as they have been throughout history. Thus, power is essential because it is needed to help states survive in the self-help system the anarchical international order creates.

We see this struggle for power in the series as well as in the real world. In the show, for example, each region in the Seven Kingdoms seeks to increase its military strength in order to protect itself from those who would challenge it and/or overtake others for their own gains. Even when power is consolidated under Robert Baratheon, it is only temporary; just as soon as a region gains enough strength to challenge the Baratheons' (and later Lannister's) claim over their territory (e.g., the North) the opportunity is seized to regain power. The same occurred when the Soviet Union saw its power diminish in 1989. The first region that retook control over its territory from the Russian government was East Germany. This act of independence was followed by states all over Eastern Europe leaving the Russian government a shell of the mammoth powerhouse it once was. States in the real world also seek power for survival—each seeking better technology, weapons, or alliances to protect itself and its interests. The United States and Russia, for example, have long been embroiled in an arms race to outpace the other's military capabilities. Iran, Israel, and North Korea also have sought nuclear technology to protect their state from outside attack and interference. In the series, the North seeks alliances with its neighbors to compete militarily, while Cersei, on the other hand, develops wildfire, and Daenerys, of course, has the power of her dragons.

The show demonstrates other elements that can be juxtaposed with the real world beyond just the parallels with war and the quest for power. For example, the White Walkers, as a threat to all mankind, could be a symbol of climate change. The various kingdoms are too busy negotiating agreements with each other or sometimes fighting for resources or the Iron Throne that they forget the inevitable doom of the White Walkers cleansing the lands of the living. Many kingdoms far south of the wall (where the White Walkers tend to reside) believe their threat to be too far away both geographically and chronologically. This compares to states not reacting to threats of severe/irreversible climate change disasters because of their loose perception of science or preoccupation with what they perceive as more pressing or dangerous threats.

The show also demonstrates the struggles female heads of state face when gaining power. Most of the female characters who hold diplomatic or military power struggle with likability among other leaders and are forced to act more masculine and traditional to gain trust and respect. We see these same developments in the real world (e.g., Hillary Clinton). Identity politics is also apparent when examining the perception those south of the wall have of the Wildlings. The Wildlings are viewed as barbaric, thieves, and murderers. It is only after we are introduced to them in the series that we learn the Wildlings view people south of the wall in much the same way. As it turns out, the threat of the White Walkers helps the two groups realize they have much more in common than previously thought.

The series mirrors the struggle between groups in society and the lack of respect for the human rights of some individuals, too; particularly, those not part of the elite groups in society. For instance, The Unsullied are slave-soldiers who are forcefully castrated, bred as eunuchs, and trained for battle in Slaver's Bay. In addition, parallel to the developed and developing world, in the series the wealthier kingdoms are drastically more advanced than the least-developed kingdoms. They consume more resources and have much larger armies. They also mostly interact with other wealthy kingdoms, often seeing weaker states as valuable only for their resources.

Importantly, the series displays key concepts which include the major theories of international relations—realism, liberalism, and constructivism. The show also shows how heads of state frame global concerns to their citizens, the different level of concern states have for human rights and the underrepresented populations in society, and, especially, how difficult it is to achieve harmony in the international system. In the series, characters survive at any cost, sometimes killing their own family members to gain power. Survival, more so than the well-being of all society, is the key interest.

The lack of a higher-power in the international system, in addition, leads kingdoms to be motivated by distrust and fear, much like what happens to states in the real world. As the Kingdom of Daenerys grew, King's Landing sought to eliminate the threat—first by attempting to assassinate its leader, then through outright war. North Korea, in our contemporary political world, is not known for upholding the agreements into which it enters, if it even enters into them at all. It is also known for blatant shows of force meant to signal its strength to its foes. Unable to trust the intentions of North Korea, states like Japan, South Korea, and the United States are motivated to protect themselves against it.

In sum, *Game of Thrones* effectively demonstrates the power of alliances and how easily the threat of force manipulates groups of people. It also offers an opportunity to explore other theories of interest to international relations, making it the perfect subject upon which to center this book. In addition, since *Game of Thrones* is a very popular series, setting a record for viewership, boasting 18.4 million viewers overall (Pallotta 2019) most people have at least heard of the show even if they have not watched. This familiarity helps make it easier to relate theories and concepts of international relations rather than using real-world examples which often require more in-depth historical knowledge (Young et al. 2018). Moreover, for those who simply do not like history or prefer pop culture, *Game of Thrones* makes it an interesting way to discuss the concepts because of its popularity.[1]

GAME OF THRONES AND THE MODERN STATE SYSTEM: AN UNLIKELY COMPARISON?

Game of Thrones is set on two fictional continents: Westeros and Essos. The Seven Kingdoms is the name given to the realm that controls most of the continent of Westeros and the islands surrounding it. Once divided among the seven distinct kingdoms (the Kingdom of the North, the Kingdom of the Mountain and the Vale, the Kingdom of the Isles and Rivers, the Kingdom of the Rock, the Kingdom of the Stormlands, the Kingdom of the Reach, and the Principality of Dorne), it was Aegon, later referred to as the "mad king," who (with the help of his sisters) conquered all of the kingdoms, except Dorne. Dorne did, however, later join Aegon's kingdom through marriage, and thus Aegon was able to consolidate power over them. The Iron Throne is where the ruler of the Seven Kingdoms sits and serves as the symbol of power over the kingdoms. It is the desire to sit upon this throne as the ruler of the Seven Kingdoms that has led to most of the wars that take place in the series.

The Seven Kingdoms is an absolute monarchy ruled by a king. An absolute monarchy is a government in which the monarch exercises ultimate governing authority over the state with no constitutional limitations, or otherwise, to his or her powers (Harris 2009). At the start of the series Robert Baratheon is the ruler of the Seven Kingdoms, though this changes many times over the course of the show. Because of the size of the Seven Kingdoms, Aegon appointed several "Great Houses" over nine administrative regions to be ruled by Lords who pledged allegiance to Aegon originally, and later Robert, Joffrey, Tommen, etc. Ned Stark, for instance, rules the North, but "bends the knee" to King Robert of the Seven Kingdoms. Ronnel Arryn, likewise, is the ruler of the Mountain and Vale, but also "bends the knee" to whomever sits upon the Iron Throne.

In return for their loyalty, the lords are granted a certain amount of autonomy to oversee their region. Below the lords in each region are vassals who swear allegiance to their lord *and* the king of the Seven Kingdoms. Each vassal may, in turn, have their own vassals, and so forth. Lady Lyanna Mormont is the head of House Mormont of Bear Island, for example. She commands her own army and provides for those within her realm. She, however, swears her allegiance to the North as well as lives under whomever rules the Seven Kingdoms, to which the North current-ly belongs. Though, it is worth noting when asked to commit her army to Stannis Baratheon's quest to take over the Iron Throne Lady Mormont replied that "Bear Island knows no king but the King of the North, whose name is Stark" (Season 5, Episode 2). This is important because it indi-cates the power the King holds over the Seven Kingdoms is not as consol-idated as would need be to ensure its ability to maintain control over the territory.

If one defines the state as an entity that maintains control over a terri-tory and its people through the legitimate use of force, as is common in international relations (Dusza 1989), then any discussion of states in this book would need to focus on the Seven Kingdoms as if it were a single power/state with King Robert the recognized ruler of the state; though, admittedly, Robert presides over a very decentralized system. If you limit the definition of a state in this way, however, you also limit explanatory capacity when it comes to making comparisons among the different re-gions and their vassals in the series. The North, for example, would need to be viewed as a separatist group within domestic society and the result-ing war between the North and King's Landing as a civil war and not an international conflict. Because we want to apply theories of state behavior at the international level, relaxing the definition of a state makes analysis at the international level possible.

Adding to the above problem, there is little consensus among disci-plines on the definition of a state with "no shortage of competing defini-tions" (Mitchell 1991, 77). Political scientists think of a state in very limit-ed terms. Realism, for instance, defines states simply as unitary, rational, and geographically based actors. Defining power in terms of relative mil-itary, economic, and even political capabilities does allow for states to have different levels of power (Morgenthau 1948); unfortunately, though, this definition lacks the ability to distinguish at what point a group reach-es the unitary, rational, and geographically based actor status. While use-ful at the international level, it does little to help think about the actions of actors who have not yet achieved this unitary, rational-actor status.

In addition, realists tend to ignore all but the great powers. Since many different people maintain control over a number of different re-gions, but with different power capabilities, it would disqualify many areas in *Game of Thrones* from inclusion in our discussion since places like Braavos, the Dothraki (before Daenerys' takeover and rise to global pow-er), the North (before the reign of Jon Snow), Bear Island, and Dorne, among others, would not rise to the level of a great power. Thus, using examples of the impact of these areas would be problematic if sticking strictly to the definition of a state conceived by realists as described above.

Definitions of the state also tend to focus on the type of institutions within a state or reduce the state to a decision-making body only. Thus, for example, if there is a lack of hierarchical institutions, some might argue a state cannot exist. This view is often considered narrow and idealist, though, because it attempts to divide the state from society with an "elusive boundary" scholars try to "fix" with the right definition. However, one could argue any group that comes together and forms a system of governing, whether it be flat or hierarchical, could be considered a state if they stake a claim to a specific territory and defend it from encroachment by others (similar to the definition set forth above). Thinking of a state from this perspective would then allow for the inclusion of a much broader array of regions from which to draw examples of state behavior.

Some argue the type, or "ideology," or institutions in a state matter when determining if an area has reached the level of statehood (Weber 1958). However, these characteristics matter to a much lesser extent than typically portrayed. An autocratic regime—a government where power is controlled by one person, can maintain strong infrastructure, institutions, and internal (as well as external) military control just like a democratic regime. Likewise, some democracies suffer from a lack of capacity, especially newly transitioning ones. Because state capacity is not dependent upon the type of institutions in place, it is necessary to broaden how we think about states if we are to use the different regions in *Game of Thrones* as representative of territorial states.

In addition, Timothy Mitchell points out, "a definition of the state always depends on distinguishing it from society, and the line between the two is difficult to draw in practice" (1991, 77). Although less of a problem when examining societies individually, it becomes particularly problematic when attempting cross-country analysis of a system where societies take on many different forms or, in the case of the societies in *Game of Thrones*, when a society has not reached a level complex enough to be comparable to the modern territorial state. On the other hand, one could rely on Max Weber's definition of the modern state as a "compulsory association which organizes domination" and seeks to "monopolise the legitimate use of physical force as a means of domination within a territory" (Weber 1958, 82). However, such a definition is limited in explaining the intricacies of government organization or even states that have renounced the use of physical force over their given territories for various political purposes (e.g., Japan and Article 9 of its constitution).

Importantly, who is to say the Kingdom of the North ceased to exist when power was "temporarily" gained by Aegon? Did Germany not encroach upon and take over other countries temporarily during WWI and WWII? After the war, borders, for the most part, were returned to their original lines of demarcation (or were redrawn to suit the victors). Thus, the states temporarily controlled by Germany did not necessarily cease to exist, but merely saw a loss of sovereignty, or their ability to rule one's self without outside interference. Some were able to regain it after the war like France and Belgium, while others like Hungary and Poland were not so fortunate having been weakened too much. The North, at the end of the series, too, reclaims its independence with Sansa Stark ruling as the sovereign queen over the territory, turning the Seven Kingdoms officially into the Six Kingdoms, thus reinforcing control by the Seven Kingdoms over the North was only temporary.

The same ebb and flow of sovereignty experienced by states after both WWI and WWII occurred to the kingdoms that make up the Seven Kingdoms. Sticking to a rigid definition of a state as set forth by Weber, though, makes discussing these areas as "states" difficult since their status changes across time throughout the series, with some gaining power (e.g., the North and the Iron Islands) while others see their power almost completely diminished (e.g., Dorne). Again, relaxing this definition to account for states at various stages of development and levels of power makes applying the theories of international relations to states in the modern state system as well as to states residing in a system that lacks the characteristics of the modern state system possible.

To that end, we define a state as "a society with some sort of rituals, traditions, and rules that can differentiate in terms of structural organization, such as levels of hierarchy, as well as capacity to project power both internally and externally" (Young 2013). This definition meets most basic assumptions about the various components that make up a state. It also makes it possible to discuss a state throughout different levels across time and space. In other words, reworking the definition of a state to include specific characteristics of differing groups allows us to discuss the societies in *Game of Thrones* as if they were emblematic of modern states.[2]

We maintain states did not exist in their present form (aka "the modern territorial state") hundreds or thousands of years ago; this does not mean, however, that the origins of the Germanic people that currently make up the modern-day state of Germany, for example, are not identifiable in some other type of societal structure prior to the modern-day state era. Moreover, Poland, Belgium, France, etc., did not cease to exist when Germany invaded. Rather, their sovereignty was temporarily lost. Moreover, just because Bear Island pledges its allegiance to the North, Lady Mormont makes it clear: Bear Island is free to rule and make decisions for itself and does not make those decisions at the pleasure of the North. Rather, it has decided, upon its own free will, to enter into an alliance with the North and join it in battles if needed, and only if Bear Island agrees to do so (see, for example, Lady Mormont's conversation with Ser Davos and Jon Snow when considering to join the North's fight against the Boltons (*Game of Thrones*, Season 6, Episode 7). This is similar to the Triple Entente among Russia, France, and the United Kingdom. While they pledged allegiance to each other, they still retained their own individual sovereignty, and could, if they so decided, refuse to honor the alliance—though, of course, some repercussions might be felt if one did.

Just because the structure of the Seven Kingdoms is a hierarchical order where power is consolidated in the Iron Throne, the reality is, the different areas see this consolidated power as temporary, and are willing to take back their own sovereignty when the time is appropriate. Thus, it makes sense to discuss these different regions as separate states. It also prevents confusion since, as the series progresses, you see the Iron Throne lose its consolidation of power over the North, Dorne, and other regions; in fact, in the last episode of the series the North declares its independence and reclaims its sovereignty free from the Seven Kingdoms. If we start with the premise that each area is its own state, then it prevents the need to change the characterization of an area from example to example depending upon at what stage in its evolution a country is when the example takes place. "Cultural evolution is not a continuous, cumulative gradual change, in most places 'Fits and Starts' better describes it" (Wenke 1999, 336). In short, states take on many shapes during thousands of years of formation just like those in the series.

FROM BAND LEVEL SOCIETIES TO THE MODERN STATE SYSTEM

The first societies were vastly different from those we find today. Before the development of fixed agriculture man primarily lived in nomadic, hunter-gatherer societies sometimes referred to as band level societies, or, as Weber describes them, charismatic societies (1946, 295–299). The Dothraki, before Daenerys becomes queen at least, has characteristics of band level societies—moving from place to place and relying on hunting (or scavenging) rather than establishing fixed farming communities. Although societies take on many shapes throughout history, at one time, all people organized themselves at this basic level (Fukuyama 2011, 59).

Band level societies have a hierarchical structure that recognize a leader with special qualities that differentiated him from the rest of the group. These unique characteristics can range from superior intelligence, trustworthiness, or strength; the individual that brought home the most game from hunting; or, in some cases, an individual who possessed some sort of supposed magical or spiritual quality (Fukuyama 2011; Weber 1946). The White Walkers are another example of band level societies in *Game of Thrones*, though since they do not talk it is hard to know how their leaders are determined. Nevertheless, while some hierarchical structure does exist, it is not as complex as those states in Westeros and Essos. The White Walkers are also nomadic, like band level societies, and have not developed fixed agriculture, though it would seem as though the reason is because they do not need to grow food to survive. They also do not have fixed settlements with permanent residences, but rather continue to roam around the area north of the wall, waiting for their opportunity to migrate further south.

The Dothraki also exhibit characteristics akin to band level societies. The leader of the Dothraki is the one who is the greatest warrior or who has earned the respect of his fellow Dothraki. If he is deemed to lose these qualities, then a new ruler replaces him, just like in band level societies. When Drogo becomes ill and falls from his horse, for example, this is seen by the other Dothraki as a sign of weakness prompting one to proclaim: "A Kahl that cannot ride cannot lead" (*Game of Thrones,* Season 1, Episode 9).

Leaders in band level societies change frequently and do not have the ability to dictate to others. Instead, they lead by example rather than authority and give advice or an opinion rather than a command. No one is under any obligation to follow his suggestion (Fukuyama 2011, 53–55; Pilbeam 1970, 12). Moreover, the ruler's legitimacy is contingent upon his ability to maintain proof of these special characteristics. Once contrary proof emerged, the belief in and, therefore, legitimacy of the ruler disappeared (Weber 1946, 296). In short, band level societies displayed some form of hierarchical structure not present before this point, though these structures still lack much capacity by modern-day comparison.

Once band level societies adopt agricultural practices, though, they form what is known as fixed settlements. This new way of organizing adds a layer of social complexity to society. Class cleavages emerge, the rule of law is established, and, importantly, fixed settlements lead to increases in population, which bring a level of complexity of its own. As fixed settlements become more involved, they also expand by taking control of new territory. As this growth continues, they became more intricate creating distinctions with the way society organizes itself. Several different types of states emerge as a result. City-states, empires, monarchies, and theocracies are just a few of the other forms of government above the band or tribal level.

The Wildlings are a good example of societies that have progressed past the band level, but not quite reached the same level of development as the more complex states on Westeros and Essos. The Wildlings have a hierarchical structure, with Mance Rayder designated as the leader of the group, or the "King Beyond the Wall." Society is much less complex than, say, the North or King's Landing, with fewer class-cleavages, division of labor, and a more equitable transition of resources throughout the society. They do have fixed settlements and have developed fixed agriculture, though some of the Wildlings still exhibit nomadic tendencies, especially when in search of safer settlements or for more resources.

The North, King's Landing, and Dorne, as well as others in the series, are much more complex than the Wildlings, Dothraki, or White Walkers. The government structure is much more rigid, with clear lines of succession, clearly defined class cleavages, and separation of labor. King's Landing, arguably the most developed of all the states, also has a large army and has clearly demarcated borders. Its economic structure is much more sophisticated than the Dothraki, Wildlings, and White Walkers. In fact, the latter three do not appear to exchange money for goods. The Dothraki and White Walkers take what they want, whereas the Wildlings, while they do cross the wall and steal from those living in the North, for the most part, live off the land, not needing to establish the same sort of levels of commerce as King's Landing.

Though each of the above groups have distinct characteristics to differentiate it as a separate type of political order, all represent the different levels and types of statehood that evolved with time. In fact, Charles Tilly argues, the different types of governments that emerged were merely "plausible alternatives" from which elites chose (1992, 1–5). If the organization controls "the principal concentrated means of coercion within delimited territories, and exercise[s] priority in some respects over all other organizations acting within the territories," then, regardless of how homogenized or centralized authority, the political unit is a state (Tilly 1992, 5). All forms of government, therefore, represent one form of a state or another (Tilly 1992, 1–5; See also Connelly 2003; Cooper 2005; Kumar 2010). Using this interpretation, it is easy to conceptualize the different kingdoms and vassals throughout Westeros and Essos as merely progressing through different levels of statehood since, it is important to note, the process of state formation is not always continuous, resulting in ever more expansion and growth.

An empire is, perhaps, the greatest expansion a state can undertake. Empires form when territorial expansion continues beyond a state's original borders into other regions or states' territories; the Holy Roman Empire or the United Kingdom are examples. Though Rome was able to reach a level that could be called an empire, Rome itself never ceased to exist as a state. The control it was able to exert over territory, however, did change.

Although an empire is a natural extension of power-seeking states, as stated, it does not represent the final stage in a state's development. Empires can weaken, causing the state to lose control over its territory. After an empire collapses, however, the state does not disappear. Instead, its capacity significantly weakens, and it also occupies a much smaller territory (whether consolidated or not). In essence, the state loses some of its capacity to project its power. For some empires, such as the Roman and Ottoman, for instance, they virtually disappeared, leaving their citizens to be conquered and/or absorbed by the new states that emerged in the fallen empires' places. Though, for the United Kingdom, they never disappeared, only lost territory and the ability to project power globally at the same level it once did.

This phenomenon occurs to the power once held by King Robert over the Seven Kingdoms. After his death, internal unrest due to the tyrannical rule of Joffrey, compounded by a shortage of food and other vital resources, as well as a challenge to the legitimacy of the heir to the throne, all contributed to the weakening of the Seven Kingdoms and the breakaway of the North and others from the power of the Iron Throne. Though King's Landing still exists and has not disappeared, the state itself has lost its ability to control territory beyond its borders. King's Landing's loss of power is comparable to the United Kingdom losing its control over its prior colonies while still maintaining control over the original territory of England, Scotland, and Wales.

In sum, though the kingdoms in *Game of Thrones* do not represent the modern state system, if we relax the definition and use the above assumptions instead, we can make comparisons between the modern state system and the kingdoms in *Game of Thrones*. Importantly, the theories of international relations help us to understand the evolution and behavior of states. It is here that the series will prove to be the most useful.

OVERVIEW OF CHAPTERS

The book is divided in two parts: one section that covers the concepts and theories of international politics and the other which explores thematic topics relevant to this field of study. Chapter 1 begins with a discussion of the different levels of analysis. Each level is related to specific characters and/or events from the *Game of Thrones* series to help provide "real" examples to which the concepts can be applied. Chapters 2, 3, and 4 cover the main theories in International Relations. Specifically, chapter 2 explains the main theories within the realist paradigm. Focus is placed on classical realism, political realism, and neo-realism. Terms like anarchy, power politics, and balance of power are also discussed. The liberal paradigm is covered in chapter 3. Chapter 4 explains constructivism, Marxism, world systems theory, and feminism.

The second section of this book, chapters 5 and 6, cover thematic topics in international relations, namely human rights and underrepresented actors or groups in politics. The emphasis of chapter 5 is on torture and violations of women's rights, and chapter 6 includes discussions on the Indigenous peoples in international politics. In each chapter, examples from the television series are used alongside real-world examples to provide context for the concepts covered.

NOTES

1. In 2015, the television series set a record for the most Emmys won in a single year with twelve, including the Primetime Emmy Award for Outstanding Drama Series. According to *The Guardian*, *Game of Thrones* is the "most talked about show on television" (Hughes 2014; Otterson 2017). It has become more popular with each new season and shattered HBO ratings records (Otterson 2017).

2. It is necessary to note this definition differs from that given to "nation." Although it defines one characteristic of a state as having some sort of ritual, traditions, and rules, this is not the same as having a shared identity or culture. Though important for state strength, it does not accurately define "state." As Walker Connor explains, a state is tangible—readily defined and easily quantified. "Peru, for illustration, can be defined in an easily conceptualized manner as the territorial-political unit consisting of sixteen million inhabitants of the 514,060 square miles located on the west coast of South America between 69 and 80 west, and 2 and 18, 21 south" (1978, 300). No mention about the identity of the people in the area is necessary to identify the "state." Therefore, a state can be thought of as the territory over which a central power makes claim to political power and is able to demonstrate that power by extracting compliance from inhabitants and recognition of this power over the territory from foreigners and other states. Nations, on the other hand, are intangible, self-defined, and consist of "a psychological bond that joins a people and differentiates it, in the subconscious conviction of its members, from all other people in a most vital way" (Connor 1978, 300–301). A popular definition in international relations of a nation is that it consists of "a social group which shares a common ideology, common institutions and customs, and a sense of homogeneity." The group may have a sense of belonging to a particular territory, though certain religious sects also exhibit these same characteristics (Connor 1978, 301–304). International relations scholars have gone to great lengths, according to Connor, to differentiate between state and nation. Nevertheless, "having defined the nation as an essentially psychological phenomenon," he argues scholars still treat the term "as fully synonymous with the very different and totally tangible concept of the state" (1978, 301).

The merger of these two terms is problematic. The more homogenous a society, the easier it is for a state to establish institutions with a great deal of capacity, though it is not an essential component for state formation. In fact, Connor surveyed 132 states and found that only 12 states, or 9.1 percent, qualified as nation-states. In "this era of immigration and cultural diffusion," he cautions, "even that figure is probably on the high side" (1978, 301–304). These two terms must be kept separate, however, as the two are distinct from each other conceptually and merging them can cause confusion when defining a kingdom or vassal as a state.

ONE

Levels of Analysis

The relations among states are complicated to say the least. Political scientists, therefore, seek ways to simplify state behavior so that it can be understood and explained. Basic theories and concepts help achieve this. One of the most common ways to analyze international relations is through the levels of analysis. These levels, first popularized by Kenneth Waltz (1959) in *Man, the State, and War,* suggest international relations can be explained through three different "lenses." These lenses help inform political scientists when building theories since each lens simplifies the variables used to explain state behavior. The lens you use to explain the behavior, though, will result in three very different interpretations of the events that took place. For example, what caused the war between the North and King's Landing in *Game of Thrones*? Did the whole thing start because Jamie Lancaster pushed Bran Stark out of the tower, leading to a series of events that caused the war between the two families? Was it because of different values between House Stark and House Baratheon that caused tensions to overflow? Or, perhaps it was the insecurity of King's Landing that led it to lash out to make certain power stayed concentrated in its hands. Each one of these explanations represents a different level of analysis from which the answer is drawn.

INDIVIDUAL LEVEL

The first level of analysis is the individual level. The individual level sees the world in terms of the moral principles of man and how those principals translate into international politics. If you explain a conflict which occurred by arguing it is a result of a person's individual actions, then you are using the individual level of analysis. Aspects of human nature and an individual's traits, like their personality, actions, perspectives, choices, or decision-making style, etc., are also considered when examining events from this level of analysis.

Theories such as classical realism and idealism rely on this level of analysis to make predictions about the world in which we live. Classical realism, for instance, explains world events and, in particular, conflict, as a result of the inherently aggressive nature of individuals. Idealists, on the other hand, argue individuals are actually peace-loving but find themselves in situations which make them act in ways opposite to their nature (e.g., war). Regardless of which perspective you believe is correct, both rely on an understanding of the individual to explain why conflict occurs.

In short, the individual level of analysis "emphasizes the critical role played by certain individuals who happen to be in the right place at the right time to exert fundamental influence on the unfolding events (Dorff, 2004, 7). Some studies have even made the connection between the importance of individual personalities of political and military leaders and major international wars (Stroessinger 2010). Depending on the leaders' personalities, they might decide to respond to conflict by taking the offensive or by resorting to defense. Explaining WWII, for example, one might argue from this perspective that if it were not for Hitler, the war never would have occurred. Thus, it is because Hitler was in the "right" place at the "right" time to change the course of events of history toward a path of another Great War. One could likewise argue, though, if it were not for the skilled statecraft of both Franklin D. Roosevelt and Winston Churchill, the war might have ended with Germany the victor or much later than it did.

Applied to the series, this level of analysis might explain the North and King's Landing's dispute as a result of Cersei's dislike for Ned Stark. She saw him as a threat and feared he would reveal her son Joffrey was not the rightful heir to the throne and that Ned would seek to replace Joffrey with someone else. As a result of Cersei's fears, tensions escalated until war broke out between the two houses. On the other hand, maybe the war is a result of a chain of events started by King Robert, his hatred for the Targaryens, and his decision to slaughter the dire-wolf owned by Sansa. Or Catelyn Stark's decision to arrest Tyrion Lannister which led to the division on Westeros. Another argument may be that Joffrey was a bad King which led to tensions between him and his people. The growing tension increased his paranoia that he would be dethroned. As a result, he lashed out at anyone who threatened his power. His decision to behead Ned Stark sparked the war between the two families. Or, maybe you believe Lord Baelish's actions which led to the poisoning of Jon Arryn set off the entire chain of events that led Catelyn Stark to seize Tyrion, sparking the tension that ultimately led to the war between the North and King's Landing. Regardless of who you believe is to blame, each of these arguments uses the individual level of analysis to explain why war between the North and King's Landing eventually occurred.

DOMESTIC/STATE LEVEL

The second level of analysis is the domestic (or state) level of analysis. The *domestic level* examines the internal characteristics of states to explain state behavior at the international level. In other words, the structure of a state's government (democratic vs. autocratic) or economic system (capitalist vs. communist), the amount of nongovernmental organizations (NGOs) within a society, public opinion, interest group activity, civil society, or even the restrictions placed on the press or freedom of speech, according to the domestic level, all can impact the behavior of a state at the international level. This level of analysis permits the differentiation of actors (states), an in-depth analysis of the decision-making approach, and the identification of "goals, motivation and purpose in national policy" (Singer 1961, 84). In doing so, it explores the processes through which states make their decisions, including the internal and external conditioning factors that influence the outcome.

Since the "countries" in *Game of Thrones* are more emblematic of a feudal system than the modern state system, it makes it difficult to discuss differences in government structures or economic systems which is required by the domestic level of analysis. Nevertheless, some comparisons can still be made to help highlight the difference and show how this level's perspective changes the explanation as to why the North and King's Landing are at war.

There exists a great difference in the culture of the North and King's Landing; not only with the way they regard the treatment of their people, but also with how they view the responsibilities and duties a leader has to his people. People in the North, or Northmen, place high importance on valor and take the burden of leadership seriously. They also adhere to a sense of justice and the rule of law. This is evident when Catelyn Stark refuses to allow anyone to kill Jamie Lannister, insisting instead he be brought to justice. Robb Stark, reflecting on his new role as King of the North, upholds these values when discussing his role. Specifically, he states a leader must provide for and protect his people, considering what is best for them, and not just for oneself. Because of the value these leaders uphold one could characterize the North as more akin to a democratic society.

Westermen—the name of those who live in the area of King's Landing, on the other hand, pride themselves on military conquest and the accumulation of wealth. Emphasis is not placed on the importance of good leadership or justice, but rather on maintaining power and dominance. One might consider this an example of how the two societies contrast, with the North looking more democratic while King's Landing is more reminiscent of an authoritarian society. Ned Stark, in particular, was concerned with the direction King Robert was taking, believing a softer, more democratic approach to dealing with foreign adversaries like Daenerys or having mercy on his own people was better than King Robert's more authoritarian stance. Ned was also concerned that the rightful heir inherits the throne after Robert's death per the lines of succession. This is more emblematic of the peaceful transfer of power that takes place per the rules set forth in more democratic societies. Cersei and Joffrey, both Westermen, though, only wanted to maintain their power and wealth, and were not concerned with whether or not Joffrey was the rightful heir. This behavior is more reminiscent of that which takes place in authoritarian societies.

This behavior has repercussions, as well. The citizens of King's Landing, because of the more authoritarian rule of its leader, turned on Joffrey, weakening his power. The North, however, experienced a surge of support from its citizens and surrounding neighbors who cited its more democratic actions as reason for their support. As a result of the North's increase in power coupled with the decline in internal support for King's Landing provided the opportunity for the North to challenge King's Landing's dominance over the Seven Kingdoms. In short, the clash of values between the two societies, the difference in opinion as to the duties and responsibilities a leader has to his people, and the actions of citizens in each society created an environment which led to the ultimate conflict that took place between the North and King's Landing.

Perhaps the conflict between King's Landing and the growing kingdom of Daenerys Targaryen was a result of a difference in the way each kingdom saw the duty and responsibility a sovereign has toward the people within their realm. King Joffrey lacked any sense of obligation to his subjects and treated them very poorly. Daenerys, on the other hand, steadily grew her empire, preparing to retake what she believed was her rightful throne of Westeros. Her impetus for this quest, she said, was a desire to improve the human rights of individuals and to create a more just kingdom. Since Joffrey and, later, Cersei, show little concern for human rights, a clash of values between the two occurred. In other words, the difference in the internal characteristics of the kingdoms led to intensifying tensions between the two. If you explain Daenerys' quest to take over Westeros from this perspective or the clash between the North and King's Landing as a result of differing governing styles, then you are using the domestic level of analysis.

When explaining why WWII occurred one must look at the specific characteristics of the major actors. Germany, Italy, and Japan were totalitarian regimes that did not adhere to acceptable forms of behavior, like the respect for a state's sovereignty or the basic human rights of individuals. Great Britain, France, and the United States, on the other hand, are democratic regimes which are built upon the basic foundational principles of the civil rights and liberties of individuals. Democratic countries also have a respect for international norms and laws, such as the right to sovereignty. "So in this view, WWII was fought to protect the freedom-loving democracies of the world, not simply" because of an individual's actions or to balance against another state (Dorff 2004, p. 7).

SYSTEMIC/INTERNATIONAL LEVEL

The last lens political scientists use to explain events in the international system is the *systemic level*, also referred to as the international level of analysis. The systemic level of analysis is the most holistic level as it encompasses the "totality of interactions which take place within the system and its environment" (Singer 1961, 80). The systemic focus allows for the study of patterns of behavior from the entire system which includes, for instance, the power dynamics of the system as a conditioning element in shaping the actions of political institutions and states. The systemic level of analysis offers the advantage of sketching a comprehensive picture of the international system. On the other hand, due to the broad focus of its approach it has difficulties in providing a detailed explanation as to how the international system influences political actors and for this reason may be regarded as exaggerating the "impact of the system" on states (Singer 1961, 80).

There are competing arguments that exist in this level of analysis. One argues that the anarchic nature of the system, where there is an absence of higher order, enables states to voluntarily "cooperate under anarchy" (Oye 1986). When states take into consideration that they cannot reach their objectives unilaterally, for instance in a situation confronting dilemmas of common interests, states have a rational incentive to develop incentives to cooperate (Stein 1982). To do so, states may "even create and maintain principles, norms, rules, and procedures" (Keohane 1989, 83) and develop regimes, such as international legal agreements.

The other argument, one that is more applicable to the series, explains that the cause of war is determined by the characteristics of the international system (i.e., anarchic) and the actors that reside within it. "The idea is simply that the system itself exerts a kind of force on the states that compels them to behave and react in certain predictable ways" (Dorff 2004, 6). For example, when viewed through this lens, state behavior can be explained by the anarchic system in which they reside. Anarchy, in this sense, does not mean chaos. Rather, in international relations, anarchy refers to the absence of an overarching government or sovereign (think "police-force"). Without a government or sovereign to keep states "in-line" and from becoming too aggressive toward one another, states live in constant fear that they could be attacked by another state.

Germany, clearly growing in power, posed a threat to its neighbors. Fearing Germany's domination, other states formed an alliance to balance against Germany's growing threat. The events that took place, according to the systemic level of analysis, would have occurred whether Hitler was in power or not. As long as Germany posed a threat to its neighbors, they were forced to act. "The decisions made by these countries were part of a broader pattern of system-determined behavior" (Dorff 2004, 6).

Using this level of analysis to explain the war between the North and King's Landing, one would argue the conflict is a result of the fear King's Landing has that the North was growing powerful enough to challenge King's Landing's right to dominance of Westeros. Since there is no international power to stop that from happening, King's Landing had no choice but to prepare for the inevitable threat the North poses. This would have occurred regardless of whether Joffrey, his brother, Cersei, or even Daenerys herself, were ruler of Westeros since, according to this level, all states behave the same as a result of the anarchic nature of the international system; the individual leader does not matter.

The same is true if you apply it to the conflict between Daenerys and King's Landing. Daenerys' growing empire and new allegiance with Jon Snow, the new King of the North, has increased the fear that the growing powers will attempt to crush King's Landing and crown a new ruler over Westeros. In this instance, again, the individual ruler does not matter, as any ruler, according to this level of analysis, would behave the same given the same set of circumstances.

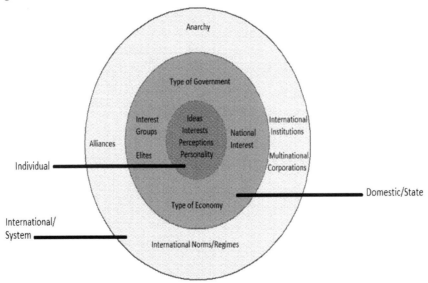

Figure 1.1.   Levels of Analysis. *Source*: **Young 2019.**

CONCLUSION

Understanding the behavior of states is complex. Fortunately, international relations provides tools through which we can simplify reality and not only understand state actions, but also make predictions about future state behavior. The three levels of analysis provide different perspectives upon which these conclusions can be drawn. As the examples in this chapter show, the lens you use determines the outcome of the explanation. Was it King Robert's actions, Jaime's, or Lord Baelish's that led to the outbreak of war between the North and King's Landing? Or, was it the conflict in values between the North and King's Landing that led to then leader of the North, Ned Stark, to attempt to weaken the power of King's Landing through the delegitimization of the heir to the throne? Or, perhaps, because the states exist in anarchy, war was inevitable regardless of who was in charge or whether values aligned or not. In short, each lens explains it differently.

TWO
Realism

Realism is one of the oldest theories in international relations. Most commonly associated with Machiavelli or Hobbes, there are quite a few varieties of realist theory. Each theory views different attributes as the key explanatory variable for understanding state behavior. Classical realists, for example, focus on the nature of the individual. Neo-realists, on the other hand, argue anarchy explains the behavior of states. At their core, though, each realist theory agrees anarchy is the driving force in relations among states. Their views are also predicated on the Westphalian or state-centric system,[1] where states are at the center of the world stage, "unconstrained by any higher political authority" (Rosenau 2018). The main difference with other theories is that realism deals with state behavior at the international level and is less concerned with the domestic politics of states on which liberalism is more apt to focus. The characteristics of a state, such as whether a state is democratic or autocratic, capitalist or socialist does not matter. Power is the key to survival for realists because of the self-help nature in which states reside.

Out of all the theories discussed in this book, realism is the one, at first glance at least, likely most associated with the series *Game of Thrones*. From a realist perspective, the wars ongoing in Westeros-Essos are a result of a struggle for power—who has it (King Robert, King Joffrey, and later Cersei) and who wants it (Daenerys, Lord Baelish, Stannis, Remi, Robb Stark, and a whole host of others!). Since there is nothing to keep another state from attacking and laying claim to one's territory (Daenerys or Stannis laying claim to the Iron Throne, for example), a self-help system is created. The survival of each state (in this case, King's Landing) is therefore dependent upon its ability to amass enough power to compete with other states (like Daenerys' or Stannis' kingdom).

Despite each theory sharing the common assumption about power and the role of anarchy, as stated above, the theories differ on how they explain the outcome of an event. In other words, the reason why the struggle for power is taking place among King's Landing, the North, Stannis, and all the others, differs depending upon which theoretical perspective you use. Below we discuss the three most prominent realist theories—classical realism, political realism, and neo-realism—using examples from the series to help highlight the differences in each.

CLASSICAL REALISM

Perhaps the Hound summed it up best when speaking to Sansa Stark as Stannis Baratheon was laying siege to King's Landing in Season 2, Episode 9: "Stannis is a killer. The Lannisters are killers. Your father was a killer. Your brother is a killer. Your sons will be killers someday. The world is built by killers. So, you'd better get used to looking at them." (*Game of Thrones*—Season 2, Episode 9). The Hound sees the world as made up of a collection of individuals whose nature it is to kill. Thus, the world will always be at war because the nature of man will never change. Classical realists share this viewpoint.

Classical realists explain the world from the individual level of analysis. According to this perspective, the individual, and, more specifically, his nature, explains the behavior of states and why wars occur. War, according to classical realists, results from selfishness, misdirected aggressive impulses, and stupidity. Self-preservation is the most important thing to individuals. Since society is a reflection of man's image, then war is inevitable unless man is changed (Waltz 1959).

It is evident throughout *Game of Thrones* that numerous individuals desire power as all compete for the Iron Throne. The death of King Robert Baratheon and the dispute over the rightful heir to the throne gave his brother, Stannis, the opportunity he needed to seek the throne, thereby increasing his dominance over the Seven Kingdoms. Daenerys sought the throne, believing it to be rightfully hers, even before Robert's death. Cersei, especially after Robert's death, can be seen throughout the series in a struggle for power. First, through her actions to make certain Joffrey held on to the throne, despite knowing he was not Robert's rightful heir. Later, with her murder of the Tyrells who she viewed as a threat to her power over her son, Tommen. And, finally, as she claimed the Iron Throne for herself after the death of Tommen. Lord Baelish, too, can be seen from the beginning strategically maneuvering his way down a path to what he hopes will eventually lead to his place at the Iron Throne. In each of these cases, it is the individual and his or her actions that lead to the events that take place.

It is not a coincidence, according to classical realism, that war is the inevitable outcome. If all men are self-interested and all reside in a state of nature that creates a self-help system, then self-preservation is key. The only way to survive is to amass enough power to protect from an aggressor. Doing so causes uncertainty among rivals causing them to also seek power. Conflict is the ultimate result (Waltz 1959).

There are two viewpoints as to whether it is possible to change man: *pessimism* and *optimism*. Pessimists believe man is born evil and his behavior reflects his nature. Pessimists argue man is defective and cannot change, thus destined to always be in a constant state of nature and fighting for survival. This explains why man is unable to cooperate and why war occurs. Optimists, on the other hand, believe war is not a given. Rather, optimists argue man can reason war is costly and, thus, it is in his best interest to cooperate. Because of this ability to reason, war can be prevented (Waltz 1959).

Regardless of whether man can reason war is costly or not, the individual is the driving force in international relations according to classical realism. The self-help system in which man resides forces him to be self-interested and seek power to protect himself. It is this self-preservation that causes war. Lady Tyrell poignantly states, "Ned Stark had many admirers, but how many stepped forward when the executioner came for his head?" (*Game of Thrones*, Season 3, Episode 4). Had anyone stepped forward for Ned, they, too, would have likely found themselves on the executioner's block. Thus, Ned, who was only trying to do the right thing by making certain the correct heir inherited the throne from Robert, was left to die with no one to come to his aid for fear of the repercussions they might face. This is a prime example of a self-help system!

Applied to states, classical realism sees individuals as making decisions to preserve themselves and their power in an anarchic world. King Robert sent assassins to kill Daenerys for fear she would grow her Dothraki Kingdom into a large threat and challenge his right to the Iron Throne. Seeing the weakened position of King's Landing due to the fight it is engaged in with Stannis, and others, King Baylon Greyjoy of the Iron Islands, takes his opportunity to attempt to seize the Iron Throne from Joffrey and conquer the mainland. Robb Stark, King of the North, compelled by his convictions to justice and in order to protect his family and way of life from the Lannisters, embarks on a war to crush the Lannisters and return the rule of law and reduce the threat to his family and kingdom. In each case, the interactions of each state are driven by the motives/desires of the individual leaders.

In sum, the war between the different kingdoms in *Game of Thrones*, according to classical realism, are a result of the actions of the different self-interested leaders vying for power in an anarchic world to preserve their own self. King Robert, Robb Stark, Daenerys, Cersei, Joffrey, Jon Snow, King Greyjoy, Lord Baelish, and all the others are the driving force behind all actions, though the state of nature in which they reside makes the actions of each inevitable.

POLITICAL REALISM

Where classical realism places an emphasis on the inherent nature of individuals, political realism focuses on the interests of states. Like classical realists, though, political realism is concerned with the state of nature. Political realists define states as unitary, rational actors aware of their external environment and strategic regarding their survival in it. For example, though King's Landing is led by King Robert, and later Joffrey, Tommen, and Cersei, political realism does not consider the different leaders as important when predicting state behavior. Rather, the system in which states reside causes all states to behave the same—regardless of who is the leader. We must, therefore, not think of the events taking place in terms of the individuals, but rather from the viewpoint of states. In other words, the North and King's Landing are competing for power. The Kingdom of Daenerys Targaryen is competing with King's Landing and the North for dominance over the Seven Kingdoms. Should Daenerys be replaced with someone else—like Jorah Mormont, for example—it would not matter. The kingdom would still be in the same fight for survival and behave the same way because of the anarchic nature of the system in which it resides.

One of the main assumptions of political realism is that states act rationally. To act rationally means that states calculate the costs and benefits of all alternative policies in order to maximize their utility in light of their preferences. Political realism also assumes states operate with full information when making decisions about their policy alternatives. When deciding whether to attack the Lannisters' forces, for example, the North weighs its options and chances for success by considering the number of troops and resources they have compared to the Lannisters. If their chance of winning the war is low, the North will rationally calculate war with the Lannisters is too costly and, thus, avoid it.

Unfortunately, just as classical realism says man can never be certain about another person's intentions, political realism argues states can never be certain about other state's intentions. This uncertainty, which Alan Collins refers to as the "uncertainty of intentions" leads to the decreased perceived security from states and ultimately fear (1995, 11–15). This fear results in a security dilemma, as states interpret the growing uncertainty as based on malign intentions. To put it more broadly, a security dilemma occurs when states seek to heighten their power to protect themselves from outside forces, but, consequently, prompts other states to do the same. The cycle continues, with one side increasing its military strength to compete with the other, until war breaks out.

Seeing the growing strength of the Kingdom of Daenerys Targaryen, King's Landing sought to increase its own military forces. This increase in power was a result of the fear of an imminent attack by the Kingdom of Daenerys. Knowing King's Landing would never stand for the growing power of Daenerys' kingdom and that it would seek to destroy it at first chance, Daenery's kingdom continues to expand its power to compete with King's Landing and ensure its' own survival in the international system.

Another reason why war is likely, according to political realism, is because bargaining is costly and yields unpredictable results because of the uncertainty that exists between states since states cannot trust each other's intentions. Even if states share a common interest, like reaping the benefits of free trade or engaging in denuclearization, states perceive the payoff for defecting from free trade or a nonproliferation treaty (NPT) as greater than the benefit of cooperation since there is a lack of trust between the actors. The prisoner's dilemma highlights this quandary.

The prisoner's dilemma is a concept used in economics to help explain why two rational individuals would choose not to cooperate even when cooperating is in their best interest. According to the prisoner's dilemma, you and your partner in crime have been arrested. The officer explains they do not have much evidence. If you both hold out, you get one year in jail. If you both confess, you each get two years. If one confesses, but the other does not, the one that confesses goes free, the other gets four years in jail for holding out. If you both cooperate, and hold out, you both get one year in jail. This is the optimal solution. The optimal solution is the choice that benefits both you and your partner the most equally.

On the other hand, if your partner confesses and you do not, you get what is known as the sucker's payoff. The sucker's payoff occurs when you make a decision that yields your partner more benefits than it does you. Because of the risk of the sucker's payoff, confessing is better for you, regardless of what your partner in crime does. Applied to states, one can see, according to this concept, it would be better off for states to cooperate and not engage in war because of the high costs. Unfortunately, a state cannot trust that another state will not attack it. As a result, it chooses to increase its power to defend itself. Other states do the same because they, too, cannot trust that other states will not also increase their power. Thus, the security dilemma occurs.

This same dilemma is applicable to states as well. If State A says it will not increase its military strength, then State B has the choice to not increase its military strength and trust State A. If it does, and State A continues to pursue an increase in its military strength, then state B ends up with the sucker's payoff—or the possibility of being outmatched in power capabilities by State A. Thus, because there is nothing to help foster trust and cooperation between the two states, State B will choose to continue to increase its military strength.

Robb Stark, the King of the North, makes a deal with Lord Frey. For passage on his bridge and agreement to align power with Robb, Robb will marry one of Lord Frey's daughters. Unfortunately, Lord Frey holds up his end of the bargain, but Robb does not when he decides to marry someone other than Lord Frey's daughter which was part of the agreement for Rob's passage on the bridge. Robb tries to make amends, offering an apology and his uncle, Edmure Tully, as a groom for Lord Frey's daughter. Though Lord Frey seems to accept this offer, he ends up slaughtering all of the Starks and their men present at what later becomes known as the Red Wedding (*Game of Thrones*, Season 3, Episode 9). He justifies his actions stating he was promised his daughter would marry a king, which she did not.

In terms of the prisoner's dilemma, Robb Stark got the sucker's payoff because he trusted Lord Frey, forgetting the number one lesson of realism—power matters. Lord Frey wanted his daughter to marry a king, giving him more power as a result of the marriage. Instead, he aligns himself with the Boltons who rival the Starks; seeing the Boltons as a better choice for increasing his power in the region. Trust is not possible in an anarchic system, according to the prisoner's dilemma. *Game of Thrones* reinforces that time and time again; the Red Wedding is just one such example.

Power, according to political realism, is the key to survival. Consequently, the concept of power is vital to understand the policy preferences of states. This is of course, even with the differences that exist between the traditional realists that view the essence of states and the concept of state interest defined in terms of power, specifically relative power (Morgenthau 1978), and the neo-realists that explain how states seek power to achieve security and will not pursue power if it challenges their survival (Waltz 1988, 625).

Power can be defined in a number of ways. The most accepted definition of power is that X has power over Y insofar as (1) X is able to get Y to do something, (2) that benefits X more than it does Y, and (3) which Y would otherwise not have done. How X gets Y to do something it otherwise would not have, though, is where the definition of power begins to get less widely accepted.

According to realism, power is defined as the particular material capabilities that a state possesses. Traditionally, material capabilities were viewed in terms of military resources. However, thanks to the increased interconnectedness of states, economic superiority (Keohane and Nye 2001; Rosecrance 1986), technology, information, and culture are also important indicators of power (Rothgeb 1993, 21–22). The components of power can even expand to include calculations of geographic distance and state objectives where, in short, the power of a state may be greater if it is exercising its capacities in a neighboring state (Rothgeb 1993). Thus, in order to improve its position in world politics, a state must either acquire more territory (which is very unlikely in the current era), exercise its capabilities in a neighboring territory (i.e., states like Russia have succeeded with the annexation of Crimea), or through economic development and trade. As a result, the concerns stemming not only from military strength, but also economic superiority (or latent power) and even geographic location, shape the policy preferences of states. How much power is enough power differs among realist theories, though.

John Mearsheimer (2001) distinguishes between two types of power—latent and military. Latent power is defined as the overall population and economic well-being of a country. Having a large population does not necessarily mean you are automatically powerful. Likewise, a country with a large gross domestic product (GDP), but with a very small population would also have very little latent power. A country must also have the resources and infrastructure in place to distribute the needed resources to the population. Dorne, for example, is a wealthy country, but is one of the least populated. This makes its latent power much weaker when compared to King's Landing who is the wealthiest and most populated of the Seven Kingdoms. The Reach, on the other hand, is the second wealthiest of the Seven Kingdoms. It is also well populated, making its latent power comparable to that of King's Landing.

Military power is nothing more than the military forces a power has in relation to rival military forces. Military power relies on latent power since you need a strong economy and a lot of people to support a large military effort. Thus, the more latent power, the better your chances of having more military power than your rivals. The Dothraki (before Daenerys rise to power) have great military power, but they lack latent power. Though they would still be a formidable foe in any fight, a sustained war would weaken them due to a lack of resources. Dorne has wealth but does not have a large population. As a result, Dorne's chances at sustaining a long war would also be difficult without forming an alliance. By the time Daenerys is ready to cross the Salt Sea to Westeros, she has amassed a great deal of latent power through her acquisition of wealth as she conquers new territory and the growing support she gains from the people who join her. Her acquisition of a large portion of territory in Essos as well as her three dragons and the backing of the Dothraki warriors give her great military power, too. Because of the latent power and military strength possessed, she is one of the most powerful leaders in Westeros-Essos. In short, the most powerful states in a system are the ones that have the largest population and produce the greatest amount of wealth. This gives them the tools needed to raise armies, gain weapons, and sustain themselves in a long war.

There also exists different interpretations of how much power is enough power. Realists, for example, view relative power as most important, whereas absolute power matters more for liberalism. Simply put, relative power is the amount of power a state has in relation to another state. In other words, a state's power only matters in comparison to the power some other state has. If X has more power than Y, then Y does not have enough power because Y has less than X. Thus, if a state is concerned with relative power, it makes the state view power in terms of a zero-sum game. This means any advantage one state gains is viewed as a loss by another state (State A + 1 = State B − 1; Gain = 0). Cersei sees the acquisition of dragons by Daenerys as a threat, for example, so she seeks to counter that threat by stockpiling an explosive called "wildfire" which is powerful enough to impose comparable damage to Daenerys' dragons. Two powers who are equally matched in their capabilities are considered to have reached parity.

Absolute power, on the other hand, is how much power a state has. Liberalism views absolute power as more important than relative power. Absolute power can include both military and economic power. From this perspective, one state's gain is not necessarily another state's loss. Rather, as long as a state's needs are met, they have no need to seek more power since the amount of power another state has is irrelevant. In other words, if X has more power than Y, but Y is satisfied with the status quo, then it has no need to seek more power since X's power is not viewed as a threat (State A + 1 ≠ State B − 1; Gain ≤ or ≥ 0).

Game of Thrones does not have a lot of examples of absolute power. At first glance it appears everyone is concerned with how much power they have and how much more they can get to protect themselves. It could be argued, though, that states have not reached a level of power to satisfy their needs. Many suffer from a shortage of food, a disregard for human rights, unsettled borders, and competing identities within a region. As a result, relative gains remain more important for most in Westeros and Essos.

Power is sometimes classified as hard power or soft power. Hard power refers to the ability to pose a threat by use of military force or other coercive tactics like economic sanctions or support of a military coup in a foreign country. The Dothraki are best known for their use of hard power, specifically their fierceness on the battlefield. They have little interest in money or diplomacy, but rather use brute force to take what they want and need to survive. Once Daenerys becomes leader of the Dothraki, she, too, understands the need for hard power. As a result, she seeks an army and eventually acquires the allegiance of the Unsullied. She uses her new army to conquer territory and gain more fighters. She also uses them to gain wealth to acquire ships and weapons. In short, she uses hard power to pursue her goal.

Though hard power is employed by Daenerys, she also uses soft power. Otherwise referred to as the "second face of power," soft power is the "ability to shape the preferences of others" through cooption (Nye 2009, 29). It can involve the propagation of culture, usage of education, diplomatic discourse, or simply the persuasion through shared values all of which can increase a state's ability to convince others to follow their objectives. Daenerys initially marches on Meereen using military force (hard power) to conquer the city. In order to solidify her rule, though, she engages in forms of soft power. For example, she agrees to marry Hizdahr zo Loraq, a Ghiscari noble of the city of Meereen. In doing so, she hopes to demonstrate a unity between her existing kingdom and Meereen, creating trust and therefore reinforcing her role as the new leader. Though it is clear she has the military strength to compel compliance, Daenerys chooses other ways to demonstrate her power and extract compliance from the people she encounters.

States can also be classified by different levels (or degrees) of power: Superpowers, great powers, middle powers, and small powers (Evans and Newnham 1998; Mearsheimer 2001). Superpowers are the strongest powers in the international system. Superpowers usually have some sort of military superiority over great powers, like nuclear weapons or an economy upon which great powers are dependent, or in the case of Daenerys—dragons. Having a nuclear weapon (or a couple of dragons), does not necessarily make one a superpower though. A state must also have the capacity to project its influence on a global scale and outmatch other states in terms of its military superiority. While King's Landing is quite powerful, it is arguably not a superpower because its reach does not extend beyond the great Wall or even parts of the North. Any influence in Essos by King's Landing is minimal and relies mainly on the use of mercenaries which prove to be unsuccessful more often than they are successful, highlighting the limitations of their powers even by these means.

At the start of the series, the White Walkers are just a small power. In fact, the only mention of the White Walkers come from the Wildlings from beyond the great Wall. They are so insignificant, though, no one takes heed until their power has grown so much they pose a serious threat to the other powers in the region. It is not until the start of the last season, however, that the White Walkers can be considered a superpower. Before then, their influence was limited to that in their region, and had barely grown to threaten others beyond its immediate region (like Daenerys' growing kingdom in Essos). By the end of Season 7, though, the White Walkers pose a threat to even the strongest states in Westeros and Essos, leading most of the powers in Westeros and Essos (Cersei being the lone exception) to form an alliance to balance against them. Though this balance of power makes the Westeros-Essos alliance a rival power to the White Walkers, you would not consider any one state alone a superpower since the combination of their latent and military power is what gives them the ability to compete.

It is not clear just how many men are in the Army of the Dead. But, if the scene from the last episode of Season 7 told us anything, it is that there are a whole lot. To be clear, the White Walkers and the Army of the Dead are not the same thing. The White Walkers are mystical beings and have humanoid characteristics. The Army of the Dead, on the other hand, are those corpses the White Walkers reanimate, also known as Wights. While the White Walkers exhibit superior intelligence, Wights appear to respond to commands from the White Walkers but lack any other signs of intellect.

The White Walkers have demonstrated their strength as a formidable power. They already successfully killed and turned one of Daenerys' dragons into an undead member of their army. The Army of the Dead also has giants which, of course, have a significant amount of strength not matched by one regular man. Wights also have superhuman strength. They also do not tire and do not feel pain. In addition, the Army of the Dead has the unique ability to continue to grow quickly, as long as there are dead bodies around. The living take a lot longer to generate new people capable of fighting in a war. This gives the undead a strategic advantage because of their reanimation capabilities. On the flip side, though, if a White Walker is killed, any Wight that White Walker made is also killed. Thus, killing the right individual can result in greater casualties for the Army of the Dead whereas if you kill any one of the humans, no one else dies as a direct result. In short, they are able to outmatch the power capabilities of any of the other great powers alone, landing them in this category.

Great powers are those powers that have strong political, cultural, and economic influence not only over others in their region, but also across the world. Developing countries never fall into the category of a great power. This is because their economic, political, and/or military power is not enough to compete with more developed states. King's Landing and Daenerys' kingdom are the best examples of a great power. Each has influence over their region but can also project their influence on a more global scale—though this does not happen for Daenerys until much later in the series. In addition, the White Walkers, by the end of the series could also be labeled a great power.

King's Landing is the most powerful state at the beginning of the series and remains powerful until the end. House Lannister has at its disposal 60,000+ ships and approximately 60,000 fighting men (Roberson 2016). King's Landing also has wildfire, a green liquid that has the same destructive capability as setting off a large bomb. No other state has a weapon as deadly as this, except for, perhaps, Daenerys and her three dragons. Their city is also fortified, abled to stave off an invasion for some time. In addition, King's Landing has shown great success on the battlefield, making them a formidable foe for anyone in Westeros-Essos.

Though Daenerys is not considered a great power at first, by the end of the series she has risen in stature as such. Daenerys' kingdom has approximately 8,000 Unsullied and 150,000 Dothraki fighters (Roberson 2016). Daenerys also has two remaining dragons; however, the White Walkers have proven that dragons pose little threat to them. They can snuff out their fire and, of course, Daenerys' third dragon was killed during a battle with the White Walkers. In fact, the White Walkers reanimated it and now have it in their arsenal (*Game of Thrones*, Season 7, Episode 6).

Middle powers, on the other hand, have influence over others within their region, but much less influence beyond. They usually have enough strength to stand on their own without needing alliances to have influence, though alliances are still necessary if facing a great or superpower. The North is the best example of a middle power. Its fighting power is significantly smaller than Daenerys' or King's Landing with around 15,000–20,000 fighters, including the Wildlings. The Vale of Arryn and Dorne are also examples of a middle power, each having around 20,000 troops, but with the capacity to raise as many as 40,000 each (Roberson 2016). Though each power alone is not strong enough to challenge a great power, by forming alliances, like the North does when it joins forces with the Vale and the Wildlings, for example, middle powers can be more competitive as a collective unit.

Small powers make up the largest group of states in the international system. These states exhibit very little influence in the international system and are commonly targeted by greater powers for domination and exploitation. We typically think of these small powers as developing or third world countries, but even developed countries who have little influence economically, diplomatically, or militarily can be a small power. Bear Island, Skagos, and Bravos all represent small powers. Bear Island, for example, has few inhabitants and a lack of resources. Though their men and women are strong fighters, they are small in number and have been battered by sieges conducted by the Iron Men and Free Folk from the Frozen Shore. Skagos is a small island, isolated from Westeros-Essos with few inhabitants and no standing army. Bravos, on the other hand, is populated and quite wealthy. While its fighting men are renowned for their skill, Bravos does not have a military with the ability to compete against the middle or great powers. All pose little to no threat to their neighbors, much less the great powers or superpowers .

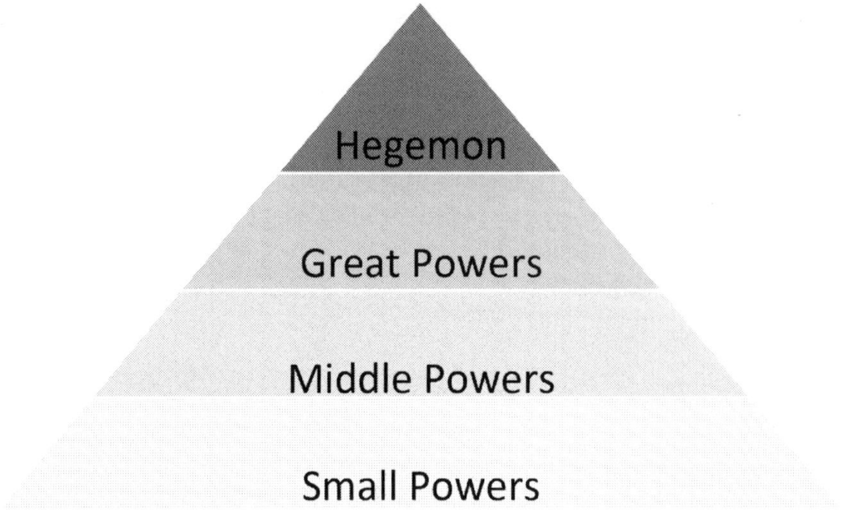

Figure 2.1.   Types of Powers. *Source*: **Young 2019.**

NEO-REALISM

Neo-realism, also referred to as structural realism, is the most parsimoni-ous of the realist theories discussed. First, it assumes states are rational actors, but that the great powers are the main actors in the international system. Small powers do not matter except for their strategic value to the great powers. The important role of the great powers is evident in the series, too. The main focus in the show is on the major power players — King's Landing, the North, the Kingdom of Daenerys, and those who yield enough power to attempt to compete with the major ones. The only time the small powers are mentioned in the show is when it is of some strategic importance to the other powers. Bear Island, for example, only becomes important when it joins forces with the North. Slaver's Bay, Astapor, and Meereen are important when they are conquered by Daen-erys.

What makes neo-realism so parsimonious, though, is that it relies on one variable to explain the behavior of states and why wars occur — anarchy. More specifically, neo-realism shifts the focus from the state of nature in which individuals exist to the anarchic international system in which states reside. Anarchy, in this sense, refers to the absence of a governing body that checks the actions of the powers within the system. Because anarchy means there is an absence of a higher authority to force states to refrain from taking advantage of others, states reside in a self-help system. Thus, anarchy results in fear and promotes the goal of survi-val. Because of the need to survive, states seek to limit the relative capa-bilities of other states. Eventually, a security dilemma occurs when, as

states acquire more power to protect themselves in the se
others become more insecure and, in turn, seek more p'
themselves. Since no one can ever feel secure in this typ
cycle continues until war occurs or a hegemon emerg₋₋
Mearsheimer 2001). In short, the lack of governance fosters fear whicn ı11
turn increases the tensions among states and the likelihood of war.

Since states understand they exist in a self-help system where survival
is dependent upon their power standing within the system, states recognize the more power they control in relation to their rivals, the less of a
threat their rivals are to its survival. States are, thus, preoccupied with the
relative capabilities of other states. This preoccupation compounds the
fear fostered by uncertainty and impacts the ability of states to cooperate
with each other because of the lack of knowledge that exists regarding
other states' preferences as well as the constant threat of conflict among
states in the system. The survival of states, therefore, mandates this aggressive behavior since the international system's anarchic nature breeds
an environment that forces states to maximize their relative power to
optimize their security (Mearsheimer 2001). In addition, those states with
the most power are free to pursue goals of self-interest with no worry
from a higher governing authority. As a result of this unchecked power
and because of their ability to hurt and at times even destroy weaker
states, states with a lot of military capability add to the uncertainty already present in the international system.

How much power a state needs depends on from which perspective
you are arguing. Offensive realists, for example, believe a state seeks
enough power to dominate all the other states in the system, or to become
a hegemon. According to this perspective, hegemonic systems are the
most stable since there is one state that has enough power to force others
to cooperate. When threatened by another state's increase in relative capabilities, though, hegemons will engage in war to stop the other state
from increasing in power and pose a challenge to the hegemon's dominance. The ability to stop other hegemons from forming, thus, is important because it eliminates the potential for competition. Defensive realists
argue, though, when power is more evenly distributed the incentives for
war decrease. This decrease occurs because when powers are more closely matched and war becomes too costly in which to engage since any
conflict would be long and result in high casualties and destruction. In
addition, because states are self-interested, there is no reason for a powerful state not to use its power to hurt or destroy its weaker rivals. Thus, for
defensive realists, only a system in which power is balanced has the best
chance of producing less war (Mearsheimer 2001).

Offensive and defensive realists also view the security dilemma differently. Offensive realists argue the security dilemma makes war inevitable
whereas defensive realists think it can be overcome if balancing takes
place. The only balancing capability in the system comes from other great

ɔwers or balancing coalitions. Again, offensive and defensive realists disagree on how much power a state needs to survive in the anarchic system; the amount of power a state has, though, determines its position in the international system (Mearsheimer 2001).

There are multiple types of systems—bipolarity, unbalanced multipolarity, balanced multipolarity, and a unipolar or hegemonic system. Each type of system provides its own level of checks and balances, or lack thereof, on states within the system. If a great power exists within a bipolar environment, for example, there is little worry of aggressive behavior as the other great power acts as a balancing force to prevent hostile inclinations. This type of system, according to defensive realists, creates the least amount of fear among the states because of the rough balance of power existing between the two great powers. Because of the diminished fear among the states in the system there is a relatively more peaceful environment overall.

Unbalanced multipolarity occurs when there are many great powers within a region, but only one potential hegemon. This particular system generates the most fear, is the most unstable, and the most prone to wars within the system because the hegemon has the greatest chance of dominating the other great powers within the region. Balanced multipolarity, on the other hand, falls in the middle of the other two types of systems. In a balanced multipolarity several great powers exist within the system, but no one great power holds the capabilities to classify as a hegemon. In other words, all the great powers have roughly the same power projecting capabilities. As a result, balanced multipolarity is likely to generate less fear than unbalanced multipolarity, but more fear than bipolarity.

Finally, a unipolar or hegemonic system is one where a single state dominates all other states in terms of power. Offensive realists argue this type of system is the most desirable for a state, as long as they are the ones that are the hegemon. Defensive realists, on the other hand, view this arrangement as unstable, since other states will constantly strive to match the relative capabilities of the most powerful state. This power grab only feeds the security dilemma making the system more prone to conflict as those with more power try to stave off those rivals seeking to challenge their position of dominance (Mearsheimer 2001).

Both King's Landing and the Kingdom of Daenerys understand survival is dependent upon its ability to quell all its potential rivals. Without gaining enough power to project itself as a hegemon with whom no one else can compete, then its chances of survival will always be in question. Though the North may not have grandeurs of world domination like the Kingdom of Daenerys, it does seek to be a regional hegemon, or a state that is more powerful than any others in its region, even if it may not be the most powerful globally. Were the North to gain enough power, though, it, too, might seek to become the new hegemon, according to offensive realists, though defensive realists would argue it would only seek to balance against the threat King's Landing poses to its sovereignty.

In sum, neo-realism explains state behavior by examining the interests of states and the calculations states make about those interests in relation to their position in the international system. War is more likely for states who feel they have nothing to lose compared to those who view the costs of war as too high. One's position in the system contributes to the cost/benefit of war. Gaining enough power to position oneself strategically within the power dynamics of the international system is, therefore, important for survival (though exactly what position within the system is the most optimal is still debated among neo-realists).

CONCLUSION

The core of realist theory is the assumption that a state of war exists among all states and societies wherein war is inevitable as a result of the potential threat from the other actors in the international system. Because anarchy results in fear, survival is the main goal of states. As a result, survival drives states to limit the relative capabilities of other states and limits the willingness of states to cooperate with one another. In sum, it is not a lack of governance that inhibits cooperation, but the lack of governance fosters fear which in turn restrains cooperation (Greico 1988, 499). States pursue security and survival as their primary goals as a direct result of the anarchic nature of the system. Self-help is therefore necessary in an anarchic order, increasing competition among states, and, thus, the potential for war is inevitable (Waltz 1986, 108).

Realists do not deny the possibility of cooperation, but instead view cooperation as a tool used by states to gain leverage, promote their own security, and advance the self-interest of states which are based on the distribution of power in the international system (Mearsheimer 1994, 13).

	Classical Realism	Political Realism	Neo-Realism
Major Actors	Individual	State	State
Human Nature	Power seeking, self-interested	Power seeking, self-interested	Power seeking, self-interested
State	A reflection of power-seeking individuals	Unitary Actor	Unitary Actor
International System	Anarchic	Anarchic	Anarchic

Figure 2.2. Theories of Realism. *Source*: Young 2019.

Specifically, according to Michael Doyle, "trade, culture, even institutions and international law [can] still exist under anarchy, but none alter its anarchic and warlike character" (1997, 209). Most importantly, no state is "prepared to engage in long-term accommodation or cooperation" but merely engages in it when necessity dictates such behavior (Doyle 1997, 210).

For cooperation and peace to exist and war to be avoided in such a system, realist theories argue a certain equilibrium, more commonly referred to as a balance of power, must be achieved. Importantly, for realists, power plays a dominant role in the formation of peaceful coexistence because of the advantage core states have to force others to take a collective stance against another adversary or on an important international issue. Moreover, powerful states can create a sense of we-feeling because of the advantage power gives them in the distribution of benefits it bestows on its allies. This we-feeling helps strengthen the alliance, further solidifying the power of the more powerful states. In other words, according to realists, peace results from deliberate actions of the state because of mechanisms such as temporary balances-of-power, the emergence of hegemonies, allegiances, and even as a result of deterrence strategies.

Jon Snow is at odds with Mance Rayder, king of the Wildlings, until both realize they must band together to fight the White Walkers. Daenerys, too, realizes she must form an alliance with the North in order to stop the White Walkers who pose a threat to both of them. Once the external threat to both of them is gone, according to realism at least, the North and the Wildlings and the Kingdom of Daenerys will turn on each other once again. Daenerys says as much when she tells Jon Snow once the White Walkers are defeated, she will take her rightful place on the Iron Throne. As we see in the final season of the series, the quest for power becomes so important to Daenerys that she stops at nothing to make certain the Iron Throne is hers (including burning the entirety of King's Landing—the very place she has been trying to rule). Just as realism predicts, cooperation for Daenerys is only a means to secure an end and power is what is most important.

NOTE

1. The Westphalian system refers to the period following the Thirty Years' War and the Treaty of Westphalia (1648), when states of Europe signed the treaty to end the war and clarified the dispute between religion, property, and authority. States, and not other authorities like the Catholic Church became the "masters of their own fates," controlling over what happens inside their given bit of territory (Rosenau and Durfee 1995, 14).

THREE

Liberalism

For those familiar with the different theories of international relations, liberalism is probably not the first theory to come to mind when you think of *Game of Thrones*. That is because, unlike realism, which focuses on power relationships, liberal theories focus more on the possibility of peace through the respect of certain values and norms. Liberalism also concerns itself with the collection and patterns of interests, the role of institutions, and the development of regimes, all of which, it argues, play a role in whether states will cooperate (Hasenclever et al. 1996). Specifically, liberal theories see interests as expanding beyond the attainment of power to encompass such things as free trade, liberty, human rights, and economic security, among others (Doyle 1997). Because of the expansion of interests to other areas than power, liberal theories, therefore, suggest cooperation is more likely than most realists believe.

Game of Thrones, especially at first, does not have a lot of examples of cooperation taking place among the different kingdoms. This is also true of the international system at one time. During the growth of the modern state system and prior to WWII the struggle for control over territory and the quest for power was prominent. Since WWII, however, there has been a much more collaborated effort on the part of states in the international system to avoid war. The creation of the United Nations (1945) and the European Union (1993) are two such examples. One could argue the feudal system in which *Game of Thrones* takes place is much more apt to engage in war than cooperation, just as the international system prior to the modern state system was much more likely to engage in war than seek a peaceful resolution compared to the modern era. This does not mean cooperation cannot occur, for there are signs of it prior to the modern state system just like there is in the series; it just means it is much more unlikely because the basic tenants needed for peace to occur, according to liberalism, have not yet been achieved.

While the quest for power never fully left the modern state system, it has been tempered through the types of mechanisms deemed so important by liberalism. For liberalism is clear, if peace is to reign over conflict and war certain variables must exist: freedom of the individual, democratic representation, private property rights, a free market, and institutions to ensure the respect of these values. Just like prior to WWII, few states have reached the standards set forth by liberalism in the series. Thus, while *Game of Thrones* does not at first appear to lend itself to the theory of liberalism, one could view the events in the international system as an example of what can happen when international institutions, economic interdependence, and a respect for democratic values and human rights are in limited supply, just as liberalism predicts.

Just like realism, within the paradigm of liberalism are many different theories. We group them as follows: Image I, which places an emphasis on human rights and international duties; Image II, which focuses on the variations in domestic society, the economy, and state structure; and Image III, which concerns itself more with the interaction of states and the effects of dyads and systems. Similar to realism, the reason why the struggle for power is taking place among King's Landing, the North, Stannis, and all the others differs depending upon from which Image you choose to explain the events.

Image I

Idealism (also referred to as classical liberalism) has its roots in the enlightenment thinkers, like John Locke. Unlike classical realists who believe man is self-interested and human nature is evil, idealists believe man is morally equal, rational, and independent. The state of nature in which man lives, though, is anarchic (Doyle 1997, 216–217). From a classical realist's perspective, Arya's nature was always evil, manifesting itself more as she grew older. An idealist, however, would argue she is not evil. As a young child, Arya lived in an environment where the things she saw and experienced forced her to change to survive. It was not that she was by nature evil, but rather her environment made her become a killer or else she would be killed herself. This is because idealists agree with classical realists that the state of nature leads to a self-help system because of the need to survive. In other words, both theories rely on the state of nature to explain one's behavior. Where idealists differ, though, is that these theorists believe man can reason that war is too costly. It is this ability to reason that allows man to overcome the state of nature and cooperate with others. Peace, not war, is the main goal of man, according to idealists. Is that, after all, not what Arya really wants—to return to the peace and happiness of Winterfell before all the tragedy began? Peace is difficult to achieve, though, because of the state of nature in which man (or in the case of the above example, Arya) resides.

As a result of the anarchy that exists, laws are needed. Within society, John Locke argues, exists a set of natural laws—or those natural rights belonging to every man. It is man's duty not to violate the natural rights of others. Even though individuals are by nature peaceful, however, the state of nature can deteriorate into conflict when laws are poorly known, partially judged, and inadequately enforced (Doyle 1997, 217–218). Therefore, a system is needed to make certain these defects do not occur and that any individual who violates these natural laws are punished. Individuals can reason that it is beneficial to submit to the rule of law if these laws are violated. As a result of this understanding, the government and society enter into a social contract with each other.

The social contract, first discussed by Jean-Jacques Rousseau in *On the Social Contract; or, Principles of Political Rights* (1762), is formed between a state and its citizens. According to the contract, the government has a responsibility to provide for the social welfare of individuals. Though individuals must give up some of their individual freedoms, they are willing to do so in return for state protection. Because the state acts as the enforcer of laws against those who violate the natural rights of man, individuals can overcome the state of nature. This type of system paves the way for cooperation and peace. If war, or as Locke refers to it, "troubled peace," does occur it is because of bias or ignorance which causes a state not to consider the implications of its actions or to be one-sided when it comes to those considerations (Doyle 1997, 219–220).

Joffrey, for example, did not uphold the social contract of the government with his people. As a result, the people rebelled, weakening his rule and making him vulnerable to outside attack. Daenerys, on the other hand, attempted to establish a social contract between her and the people she conquered, or at least eventually after seeing the repercussions when she did not in Slaver's Bay and Meereen (and until she went mad like her father in the final season). While she employed it, at least, the social contract helped her prevent further rebellion and solidify her position as the ruler of the people.

The Starks of Winterfell, also, practice the principles of a social contract between them and their subjects. The Starks view justice, the rule of law, and behaving as a good leader as important, and, as a result, the North is a peaceful state where its leaders receive admiration from their subjects. This is evident when Robb Stark can raise an army of followers to seek justice for the wrongdoings of King's Landing. Jon Snow's admiration from his subjects is so apparent it is partially why Daenerys goes mad in the final season. Again, it is the North's willingness to abide by the rule of law and enforce compliance on those who might violate those laws as well as their respect for the rights of individuals that results in the North enjoying a very different environment than that which exists in other areas, like Meereen and Slaver's Bay (at least before Daenerys' reign). The Starks' understanding of the social contract is in sharp contrast to how Joffrey, and later Cersei, of King's Landing view their duty to uphold the contract as well. In fact, when, at her wedding to Joffrey, Queen Marjorie offers the leftovers from her wedding feast be given to the poor, Cersei demands they be given to the dogs instead (*Game of Thrones*, Season 4, Episode 2). Since Joffrey and Cersei do not uphold the social contract leaders must adhere to with those whom they rule, it is no wonder, then, unrest and feelings of threat to their power occur.

The main difference between idealism and the other theories of liberalism is the level of analysis from which it views the world. Other theories of liberalism point to the internal characteristic of states or the anarchy in which states reside as the explanation for why wars occur. Like classical realism though, Image I theories explain the events that take place in the international system from the individual level of analysis; focusing specifically on the nature of man and the environment in which he resides. From this perspective, then, the wars that take place in Westeros-Essos can be explained by the actions of the men and women who lead the countries involved.

Though she may not have exhibited the signs of an evil person as a child, a realist would argue, it was obviously in Arya's nature because she is now a killer who keeps a list of those she intends to kill. In fact, there were probably signs that, at first, you missed. Arya always liked to fight and instead of learning to sew, she trained to fight with a sword. So, perhaps, Arya was not as innocent as she seemed, and evil was in her nature after all. Idealists, though, would argue Arya's environment drove her to behave the way she did, and given time and a change in circumstances, she would return to her good nature.

Joffrey, as another example, is portrayed from the start of the series until he meets his untimely demise on his wedding day as evil. His brother, Tommen, though, does not have this same evil tendency. Why, then, did one turn out evil while the other did not? A simple argument might be because Tommen did not face the same environment as his brother since it was his brother, Joffrey, who was always destined to be the king. Since Tommen did not face the same threat to his survival his behavior was different. Given time in his role as king, Tommen, too, would have developed the same power-driven nature as his brother, Joffrey. This is not necessarily because Tommen was by nature evil, but, importantly, as idealists argue, because there was a lack of enforcement against those who violated the natural laws governing man. With democratic representation, Joffrey could have been removed from office instead of reigning as a sovereign over his people. With Joffrey removed, his policies, too, are removed, allowing for a more congenial leader like Tommen to take his place. Because there was a lack of democratic representation, Joffrey and his abuse of power could remain. In short, it is not that human nature would have taken over and led Tommen down the same path as Joffrey; rather, Joffrey behaved the way he did because of the lack of important tenants in society, like the respect of the natural rights of man, the presence of democratic representation, or the adherence to a social contract.

Importantly, idealists do not discount the need for war. They do, however, distinguish between "just" and "unjust" wars. If "any aggressor state . . . violates the natural rights of states or individuals" then it "makes itself the target of a just war of defense and even conquest" (Doyle 1997, 220). Wars, thus, act as the same enforcement mechanism at the international level that punishment for violation of laws do at the domestic level. The Starks are seen throughout the series as arbiters for these principles. Ned Stark was a firm believer in the rule of law within his own region, the North. He felt it important to instill these same principles upon his children. When a deserter from the Night's Watch must be punished and, therefore, executed, Ned Stark takes Bran to watch explaining it is his duty, as the Lord of the North, to make certain that he is enforcing the laws by which his subjects are supposed to live (*Game of Thrones,* Season 1, Episode 1). And, when Ned feared the rules of succession were being violated upon King Robert's demise, he acted to right the wrong, which ultimately cost him his life (*Game of Thrones,* Season 1, Episode 10). Because of Ned's execution, Robb Stark, Ned's heir, waged what he felt was a "just" war against King's Landing for this unjust act, as well as for Joffrey's failure to uphold his social contract with his subjects (*Game of Thrones,* Season 2, Episode 1). These wars would be considered just wars since they were fought to right a wrong that violated the international rules set forth. Stannis' war against King's Landing, however, would be considered an unjust war since it was, presumably, a grab for power and not as a result of some violation of established international rules.

For Image I theories, like idealism, in short, the world is not fixed in a battle of evil versus evil where only the strongest survive. Rather, peace is the goal of individuals. Unfortunately, the state of nature is tenuous and can fall into such a state that peace can be threatened. Creating mechanisms to make certain this fall does not occur is important to foster peace. Submitting to a social contract between a sovereign and its subjects as well as transferring these same principles to guide states in the international system can create the environment needed for peace to prevail.

Image II

Where realism sees states as unitary, rational actors, liberalism argues states are not unitary nor rational actors, but are rather made up of a set of internal characteristics that shape their actions at the international level. Whether the state is a democracy or communist country, its economic system, the number of nongovernmental organizations (NGOs) within a country, special interest groups, and even corporations within society, among others, all shape a state's preferences. State behavior reflects these preferences.

Because realism and liberalism disagree on what shapes a state's preferences, this means they also disagree on what is most important for states. According to realism, all states share the same preferences (the quest for power), making them homogenous. Liberalism, however, argues state preferences differ. Some states may seek power, whereas others are more concerned with domestic matters or economic prosperity. King's Landing, for example, wants to maintain its power over the Seven Kingdoms. The Dothraki have no desire to rule over all of the kingdoms but want to retain their lifestyle and dominance over their territory. Braavos, founded by slaves, is a thriving merchant city and home to the Iron Bank. It is also the world repository for gold. Its' preferences are, therefore, to retain this economic position, which is much different from the preferences of King's Landing or the Dothraki.

Since states do not have the same preferences, their cost/benefit analysis of what they need to survive also differs. As a result, state behavior at the international level will also be different. For some states, like King's Landing or the Iron Islands, power may be the most important thing to them; therefore, their actions are a result of this preference. Other states may view economic power as more important. Qarth, for instance, is more concerned with trade to sustain its economic prosperity. War is viewed as costly and, thus, their preference is to avoid it if possible.

Another assumption of liberalism is the important role economic considerations play when it comes to state cooperation. Commercial Pacifism, for instance, argues market societies are fundamentally against war for two main reasons. First, elected officials are constrained by their citizens when it comes to declaring war. This constraint stems from the fact that citizens are the ones bearing the burden of fighting on the front lines of a war and more likely to feel the direct and indirect costs; these include everything from dying on the battlefield to paying more for petrol for their automobile. As a result, citizens are less likely to support a war than their leader who sits behind his desk more immune from the consequences.

Second, wealth satisfies human interests and, according to Adam Smith, "if well organized, [can] contribute to moral perfection" (Doyle 1997, 232). A state based on the values set forth by liberalism that also adopts a laissez faire market system will see a natural progression toward improvement because these types of systems encourage "the efficient production of a division of labor and it induces individuals to consume and produce in ways that rationally adjust their activities to the intensity of their effective demands for goods versus money, work versus leisure, security versus risk, and present versus future consumption"

(Doyle 1997, 232). The market system also "brings 'perfection' by allowing the exercise of moral liberty—the freedom to choose—in a civil society" (Doyle 1997, 233). Because this type of system allows individuals to pursue their own interests free from the shackles of a dictator or feudal lord while ensuring individuals' needs are satisfied, peace is much more likely.

In addition to the benefits of individual cooperative exchanges at the domestic level, economic interdependence among states at the international level also promotes cooperation. Simply put, if Country A grows cotton and Country B makes wine, and County B needs Country A's wine and Country A needs Country B's cotton, then both are more likely to cooperate with each other provided they cannot get these goods from somewhere else at a comparable price. In other words, states are interconnected in the modern era, linked via their economies and even culture. The cutting of ties from another state may not equally impact each state, but it will have a negative impact on both nonetheless. As a result, cooperation is preferable. The economies of the United States and China, for example, are so interconnected it is unlikely conflict between the two would occur, not just because of the severe military causalities that would result, but also because of the devastating impact it would have on each state's economy.

Though trade does take place among the different kingdoms, there is limited evidence of economic interdependence among them. While some areas specialize in certain goods (the Reach, for example, is known for its wine and lush fruits whereas the Vale predominately produces scented candles, pumpkins, wheat, corn, and barley), the series does not present the different areas as dependent upon one another. The fact that there is no real evidence of economic interdependence in *Game of Thrones* actually helps highlight liberalism's argument that economic interdependence promotes a more cooperative and peaceful environment, though. Since economic interdependence is lacking in Westeros-Essos, it is no wonder, liberalism explains, war is so common.

The promotion of absolute gains through free trade, human rights, and the promotion of economic equality is important for fostering cooperation. To paraphrase a quote from Elle Woods in the film *Legally Blonde* (2006), "Happy people don't kill [people]. They just don't." Tyrion agrees when trying to reason with Joffrey over the treatment of his people when he says, "It is easier to rule happier subjects than angry ones" (*Game of Thrones,* Season 2, Episode 6). When an individual's needs are met, including not just food, clothing, shelter, and other basic necessities, but also when they are treated with dignity and respect and as an equal in society, their level of "happiness" goes up. Happy people are less likely to engage in conflict. In fact, some of the happiest states in the world are also the most peaceful. For example, the World Happiness Report, released annually by the United Nations Sustainable Development Solutions Network, ranks Finland as the happiest country on Earth.[1] In addition to having an abundance of green space, high environmental standards, and a high standard of living, it is also considered the most peaceful place on Earth. Norway and Denmark rank second and third on the list and share these same qualities. The correlation between happiness and peace is not surprising for liberalism, since one of its core assumptions rests on states upholding these values in order to achieve peace at the international level.

In *Game of Thrones,* few countries have reached a level of satisfaction comparable to Finland, Norway, or Denmark. Not to mention, Finland Norway, and Denmark enjoy residing in a relatively stable and peaceful international system, at least within their immediate area. Few in *Game of Thrones* have that luxury. The Vale, though, comes close. It is extremely prosperous and serves as the major trade center of Westeros with Essos and the Free Cities. Though it does maintain military power and has engaged in war before, the Vale is known for its neutrality. As a result of these characteristics, it is often compared to Switzerland (Satran and Chiaramonte 2017). It is important to note wealth alone does not bring happiness and peace. The Westerlands are the wealthiest region in all of Westeros-Essos. However, because inequality among groups in society is rampant, the requirement that the needs of society be met is not fulfilled which explains why it is far from a peaceful state.

States must also respect human rights and establish regimes which uphold the rule of law and the rights of individuals. These institutions, according to liberalism, are essential to make certain peace prevails. One of the main assumptions as to why this relationship exists is that institutions promote juridical equality by guaranteeing private property rights. Any violation of an individual's rights results in punishment. As a result of the threat of punishment, there is an incentive to comply. These assumptions harken to Rousseau's Social Contract, but whereas Image I theorists view human nature and the state of nature as the important variables that explain war, Image II theorists focus more on the internal characteristics of states. Institutional differences, specifically with the way they are arranged to provide for the protection of individuals rights (or not) is the important explanatory variable. Democracies, for example, inherently possess the type of institutions needed to uphold the values necessary for the promotion of peace. Autocracies, which do little to protect individual rights, on the other hand, are more likely to produce conflict and war. Not only do "happy people not kill people," but because there are mechanisms in place to hold leaders accountable in democratic societies, they are less likely to engage in war. Since autocracies do not have the same concern about the burden war will place on its citizens, war is much more likely (Doyle 1997, 205–208).

In addition to the promotion of a free-market system and the establishment of democratic governments and the respect for human rights, diplomacy, rather than power politics, promotes cooperative behavior according to liberalism. Realism would argue diplomacy works best when you have military power to back it up. Without it your bargaining leverage is severely weakened. George Kennan once said, "You have no idea how much it contributes to the general politeness and pleasantness of diplomacy when you have a little quiet force in the background." It is important to note, though, Kennan referred to the force as a "quiet" one. In other words, the focus should still be on diplomatic efforts, and "not simply on blowing things up." To put it another way, carry a big stick, but speak softly while doing so (Walt 2013, para. 11–12). The Cuban Missile Crisis provides an example.

October 1962 could have seen the start of WWIII and, quite possibly, the first nuclear war. Instead, it turned out to be one of the greatest examples of diplomacy prevailing over power politics. Kennedy had several options, among which was a full-scale ground invasion of Cuba and/ or the use of strategic air strikes. These options were considered too costly because of the likely nuclear retaliation from the Soviet Union leading to the potential for mutually assured destruction. Instead, Kennedy decided to engage in aggressive diplomatic talks with Soviet leader, Nikita Khrushchev. At the same time, the United States sent its ambassador, Adlai Stevenson, to the United Nations to present its case against the Soviet Union and ask for diplomatic pressure to be placed on the Soviet Union by the other member nations. Even the naval blockade by Kennedy was called a "quarantine" in order to de-escalate the perception by the Soviet Union that the United States was escalating tensions by increasing its military efforts. When the USSR's ships passed the quarantine, Kennedy ordered the line be brought back to avoid having to use force on the ships. All the while, he continued to maintain a line of communication with Khrushchev, brokering terms for the withdrawal of the missile in Cuba in return for the United States' withdrawal of its missiles in Turkey. It was through these direct communications as well as the diplomatic pressure placed on the Soviet Union at the United Nations that the crisis was tempered and war avoided.

After the battle at the wall in Season 4, Episode 9, Jon Snow enters the camp of Mance Rayder and says he wishes to engage in diplomacy. He also approaches Daenerys wishing to engage in diplomacy and build an alliance between the two countries. In both of these instances, Jon Snow is successful in building a bridge between two opposing sides to come to an agreement on terms for peace. A realist, however, would argue Snow only engaged in diplomacy because it suited his own self-interest. For example, the Night's Watch had lost most of their men. Threatened with another attack from Mance, Jon Snow decided to engage in diplomacy. Had his men been at full strength, he would not have chosen diplomacy or tried to cooperate. The same is true for Daenerys. According to realism, he sought an alliance with Daenerys not because he wanted to prevent an impending conflict between the North and her kingdom, but because it was in his self-interest to do so since her power would give him a chance to survive the inevitable war with the White Walkers. And, the only reason Daenerys agreed to align with Jon Snow was because she knew the White Walkers posed a threat to her if she did not. Since both liberalism and realism are just theories, it is hard to say for certain which explanation is correct.

Image III

Neo-liberal institutionalism stresses the importance the anarchical nature plays in dictating state behavior. But, unlike realists who see peace achieved through strategic, rational, and deliberate calculations of the state, neo-liberal institutionalism argues it is through the construction of institutions that cooperation, the furtherance of the common interest in survival, and trust among the members in the community are formed. In fact, according to neo-liberalism, the key to enhancing stability is the proper management of military power through institutions (like the League of Nations, NATO, WTO, or the UN, for example).

It is through the construction of institutions that cooperation, the furtherance of the common interest in survival, and trust among the members in the community are formed. Specifically, neo-liberal institutionalists argue, institutions contain norms and provide mechanisms that make states accountable to each other, lower transaction costs, and provide members with a common set of interests. Institutions facilitate international cooperation, not necessarily by changing an actor's preferences, but by altering a state's incentive (or costs) for taking an action to secure those preferences. Institutions also help reduce a state's information costs associated with negotiating, monitoring, and enforcing agreements and raise the cost of noncompliance.

Consider the prisoner's dilemma. As you recall, the two prisoners do not trust each other and therefore decide to defect and not cooperate with each other for fear of receiving the sucker's payoff. Both end up with the suboptimal outcome. However, according to liberalism, if there was something that bound the two by a common set of values, norms, or forced compliance as a result of institutional constraints, then both prisoners would cooperate. For instance, if both were members of the mafia, they would know the penalty for squealing is high—one ends up "swimming with the fishes." There would be an incentive to trust the other because the cost associated with them defecting and squealing is too great. Thus, because of the network of international institutions underpinned by strongly supported norms and rules fostered by the institutions, the anarchical condition of the international system can be overcome, and peace and stability are possible.

In *Game of Thrones* you see attempts to instill institutions and norms which guide the behavior of individuals and states. The Iron Bank could be considered equivalent to the World Bank or IMF, with each lending money to states to further development (albeit in some cases in *Game of Thrones*, like that of King's Landing, that development occurs through funding efforts to wage war). Both the World Bank and the IMF set forth specific terms to which states must agree, thereby forfeiting their sovereignty to the institution and agreeing to a set of standards (or rule of law) by which they must adhere.

There also exists, for example, an accepted international norm among most states in *Game of Thrones* that "trial by combat" is a legitimate form of justice. The best example occurs when the king of Dorne's brother, Prince Oberyn, is killed when fighting on behalf of Tyrion at his trial by combat in Season 4, Episode 8. In Season 5, Episode 2, "The House of Black and White," Prince Oberyn's lover Ellaria Sand is speaking with King Doran Martell about the death of Oberyn. She seeks revenge for his death, but the king reminds her that his brother died as a result of trial by combat which, by law, is an honorable death. Had this norm that death by trial by combat not only been legal, but also an honorable way to die, then it is possible some sort of conflict might have occurred between Dorne and King's Landing. Because of the institutions and norms in place governing this type of behavior, conflict did not occur.

Like neo-realism, neo-liberalism views the relationship between state behavior and the basic causal variables underlying state preferences as exogenously driven. Cooperation determines state behavior which, in turn, alters the structure of the international system. This view differs from neo-realism in that, according to neo-liberalism, institutions can be a driving force motivating state behavior. Moreover, according to neo-liberalism, institutions can independently change state behavior and lead to peace. It does this by convincing states to reject power-maximizing behavior by helping to facilitating trust. Importantly, institutions can induce cooperation and reduce conflict by overcoming the collective action dilemmas which result from the lack of any overarching enforcement authority. Thus, as a result of the network of international institutions underpinned by strongly supported norms and rules fostered by the institutions, the anarchical condition of the international system can be overcome, and peace and stability are possible (Keohane 1989). The fact Dorne did not attempt to avenge the death of Oberyn is an example of the impact of institutions on state behavior. Realism, though, would argue the reason why Dorne did not attack King's Landing is because it knew it could not compete with King's Landing's power capabilities.

Finally, according to neo-liberalism, liberal institutions and principles create a pacifying effect and peace is achieved because it creates an "unwarlike disposition." Because only a minority of the population gains from wars, democratic societies are unwilling to pursue the interests that a majority of the population does not hold. Peace among states is possible even in the anarchic society as a result of the social constraints placed on leaders by the people they rule. Kant's liberal internationalism claims as republics emerge and as culture progresses the rights of individuals are understood. The emphasis placed on legitimate rule of the people, leads rulers to take more cautious policy approaches, avoiding war, and setting up the moral foundations for the liberal peace. Moreover, because republics exercise democratic caution and recognize the international rights of other republics, peace is fostered further.

Thus, although states continue to live in international anarchy, in the sense that there is no world government, it is possible to tame this anarchy and make it subject to the rule of law resulting from the creation of liberal institutions. Some even argue a world full of democracies would be the most peaceful. Democratic peace theory, drawing from Kant's liberal internationalism, argues democracies are inherently more peaceful than other forms of government. As a result, if peace in the international system is to exist, democratic regimes must be established.

Democratic peace theory makes several assumptions about democratic regimes and the international system which mirror Kant's. First, democratic leaders are forced to accept culpability for war losses to a voting public. As a result of this accountability, leaders in democratic regimes establish diplomatic institutions for resolving international disputes rather than resorting to more aggressive, warlike tactics. According to the selectorate theory, for example, democratic nations do not go to war with other nations unless they are certain that they can win, and if they do engage in war, they engage in war with all available resources to ensure the likelihood of victory. "This was shown to follow," according to Bruce Bueno de Mesquita and colleagues, "because as the winning coalition gets larger, the prospects of political survival increasingly hinge on successful policy performance" (2004, 263). Thus, political leaders in democracies have a greater incentive to ensure military victory. In the last episode of the series, for example, Samwell Tarly suggests creating a system whereby the people select their own leaders. The implications being if the leader failed to treat his or her subjects appropriately, they could be removed from office. He was, of course, laughed at by the rest of the council (Season 8, Episode 6, "The Iron Throne"). Nevertheless, his suggestion encapsulates the argument democratic peace theory makes: leaders who are accountable to their subjects/citizens will be better leaders who work harder to achieve peace than to gain power to wage war.

In the converse however, autocracies—those nations with small winning coalitions—are more likely to engage in war because the threat of losing office is minimal as long as the leader does not squander so many resources that the gains of the winning coalition are significantly diminished. Thus, democracies make unattractive targets quite simply because of the effort they exude in fighting military battles. Therefore, according to selectorate theory, the reluctance of democracies to go to war with each other is a result of strategic policy choice on the part of the leader to preserve his position and not as a result of common value systems and shared norms as generally assumed by democratic peace theorists (Bueno de Mesquita et al. 2004, 264).

Another assumption of democratic peace theory is that liberal democracies externalize their domestic norms of conflict resolution. In addition, there exists mutual trust and respect between democracies, especially when democracies are faced with an eminent conflict. In other words, democracies adopt a set of similar norms regarding their behavior when it comes to resolving disputes. Because democracies all adopt these norms, democratic states are less likely to view other democratic states as hostile. In addition, leaders in democratic regimes are slow to mobilize when it comes to war because of the system of checks and balances that exist within democracies. This system limits a democratic state's ability to execute surprise attacks and encourages democracies to reveal private information about their level of resolve (Russett 1993). This level of transparency helps facilitate trust and cooperation in the international system.

Finally, liberal democracies tend to adopt capitalistic systems. In addition to the reasons already set forth above about the benefits economic prosperity and capitalistic systems have on the promotion of peace, democracies also tend to possess greater public wealth than other states because of these systems. This increased wealth occurs because capitalistic systems promote free trade which is better at fostering economic growth compared to other systems. Communist systems and other autocracies, for example, tend to avoid free trade and are often stagnant or suffer from economic inefficiencies and greater income inequality between the leaders and their subjects. As a result of this increased wealth experienced in democracies, democratic societies have a greater interest in preserving their infrastructure and resources than autocracies that tend to be less prosperous. War, thus, becomes too costly to pursue for democracies yielding greater chance for peace (Russett 1993).

Critics of the democratic peace theory, of course, argue there is "good reason to doubt that joint democracy causes peace." Rather, the likely cause of peace between democracies can be found by examining the dominant relationship of the United States which creates an imperial peace that is mistaken for the democratic peace (Rosato 2003, 599). Erik Gartzke argues it is not a democratic peace that exists, but rather a capitalist peace. Economic development, capital market integration, and shared foreign policy preferences all play a contributing role in the explanation for decreased international conflicts and wars. Specifically, Gartzke finds the peace that exists between democracies also exists between capitalist dyads (2007, 180). Constructivists, on the other hand, a theory we will discuss in the next chapter, would see the value of sharing similar norms as the cause of peace, further arguing autocracies are just as likely to not go to war with each other because of the shared values and norms they too possess. Nevertheless, according to liberalism, by establishing cosmopolitan law and a pacific union, states will inevitably establish a peace among themselves thus overcoming the dangers posed by an anarchic system. Until there is a world full of democracies, though, it is difficult to know if world peace would be achieved under these conditions.

	Idealism	Liberalism	Neo-Liberalism
Major Actors	Individual	State	State
Human Nature	Peace seeking	Peace seeking	Peace seeking
State	A reflection of individuals	Unitary Actor	Unitary Actor
International System	Anarchic	Anarchic	Anarchic

Figure 3.1.   Theories of Liberalism. *Source*: **Young 2019.**

CONCLUSION

According to liberalism, the dynamics of cooperation are best understood by examining the effect of structure on cooperation as well as the interactions that take place between actors in world politics. Although cooperation is hard to achieve, the ability to link issues and the willingness of actors to practice reciprocity can increase the level of cooperation among actors. Moreover, actors' perceptions, shared preferences, the number of actors, and the concern regarding the future also directly impact and account for the level of cooperation, or lack thereof, under anarchy. Finally, to facilitate cooperation in world politics actors should establish hierarchies and international *regimes* (norms, rules, principles and decision-making procedures) that help to reinforce, institutionalize, and foster cooperative behavior among states.

Realists disagree with the potential for institutions to foster cooperation and decrease the potential for war. Instead realists argue, institutions are just a reflection of the interests of the strongest states. One of the key arguments of institutionalists is the ability of institutions to settle distributional conflicts. This role does not conflict with traditional realist perceptions of balance of power logic. Instead, institutions ensure agreements reflect the balance of power. Moreover, issue-linkage and the facilitation of bargaining—two important attributes used to support the necessity of institutions—do not contradict realist assumptions. Although institutions are helpful in this regard, bargaining and issue-linkage existed in world politics before institutions came on the scene.

In sum, while institutions can play a role in facilitating cooperation, this function is not enough to create an environment that reduces the outbreak of war according to realists. The balance of power is still the most important component in the international system since states can never be certain about other states intentions. Because of this uncertainty, states are constantly involved in security competition resulting from the fear the great powers have regarding the unknown intentions of other state actors. Because of the fear generated by the increased security competition resulting from the uncertain environment in the system as well as the constant struggle for increased power capabilities, power maximization continues which in turn triggers even more fear resulting in even more power maximization, and so on, until either war breaks out or a potential hegemon emerges. Liberalism, however, believes the establishment of democracies and the reliance on institutions can help states overcome the self-help system and avoid war.

NOTE

1. The report ranks 156 countries across six factors including GDP, life expectancy, social support, generosity, freedom, and corruption. The 2018 report, for the first time, also assessed the happiness levels of immigrants in 117 countries.

FOUR

Critical Identity Perspectives

The first debate that took place in international relations was in the 1930s and 1940s between realists and idealists. The debate sparked as a result of the skepticism of realists to the idealist optimism "of cooperation in international politics through legal agreements and the building of international institutions" (Tickner 2001, 22). Some argue this debate was not necessarily a debate within international relations but was an evolution from international law and institutions to the study of international politics. The second debate occurred during the 1950s and 1960s when realism was charged by more scientifically oriented scholars as lacking scientific credibility. As a result, scientific research programs were developed that built upon realist assumptions in order to conduct systemic and cumulative scientific research in the hopes of diminishing the likelihood of future conflicts between states.

The third debate in political science has taken place between positivists and postpositivists and encompasses a variety of critical approaches such as constructivism, postmodernism, and historical sociology. All these theories challenge "the value of social-scientific theories for understanding world politics" and debate the validity of rationalist and reflectivist epistemologies (Tickner 2001, 26). Specifically, this focus is more concerned with the role of agents and not just with the impact of structure. Arguing neither is "fixed" or "static" as realism or liberalism claims, but rather each works to shape the other making individuals, states, and the system in which they reside malleable. As a result of this competing viewpoint with the long-held assumptions made by both realism and liberalism a new paradigm in political science emerged called the critical identity perspective.

Theories within the critical identity paradigm typically explain events using the individual level of analysis. For these theorists, the individual (agent) plays a pivotal role in the outcome of events that unfold in both domestic and international society. That is not to say the environment (structure) in which an individual resides does not impact his/her behavior. In fact, the relationship is reciprocal with an amalgamation of variables playing a role. Out of the interaction of all these variables form norms, interests, ideas, institutions, and even regimes which, in turn, inform the behavior of individuals. Understanding the development and impact of these variables is as important for critical identity theorists as understanding power is for realists.

Critical identity perspectives are also concerned with the imbalance among groups in society and the social construction of knowledge. Knowledge, in this sense, is a mere reflection of a process that has led society to accept something as true even though, in reality, it may merely be constructed in a way that serves the most powerful (Cox 1981). Max Weber, for example, argues religion, specifically that rooted in Calvinism, encouraged the development of the modern capitalist system. According to Weber "Worldly achievement . . . both glorified God and was a sign that an individual was to be blessed in the afterlife. . . . For Protestants, the subjective probability of reaching heaven is assumed to be increasing in the wealth an individual accumulates during his lifetime" (Cavalcanti, Parente, and Zhao 2006, 127). This viewpoint creates a society of complicit individuals who do not question their current conditions. In short, society is molded so that some individuals benefit more than others, and so that those that do not benefit do not question their plight. It is not, as realism might argue, a system in which one's fate is inevitable because of where he/she resides or as a result of who has the most power; rather, the system is constructed through the actions of individuals.

The system in which individuals reside further enforces the norms constructed in society. Rules are put into place to protect acceptable forms of behavior which have already been established by norms in society. Since both are constructed, however, both can also be deconstructed, or shaped, in such a manner so that groups in society are more equal. Applied to international relations, the argument remains the same. Great powers have shaped the international system in such a way that it benefits them. Since the international system has been constructed this way, though, it, too, can be deconstructed and reorganized into something that is more equal and, thus, peaceful.

Critical identity perspectives provide an alternative way to view state relations that go beyond the traditional approaches that focus more on the material capabilities of states and the unchangeable nature of the international system. Though not all critical identity perspectives are the same (for example Marxism is more concerned with the social construction of classes in society, feminism explores the role gender plays in international politics, and world systems theory concerns itself with the inequality among states at the international level), each draws from the assumption that the world in which we live is socially constructed and, therefore, can be reconstructed to become more peaceful.

In this chapter we explore some of the more prominent theories that fall within the critical identity paradigm: constructivism, Marxism, world systems theory, and feminism. Each theory demonstrates how the above assumptions regarding the role of agency and structure and the implications each has on imbalance within society are prominent, even though all apply the assumptions in different ways to address a variety of questions.

CONSTRUCTIVISM

"What is it you want, exactly?" Tyrion asked. "Peace, prosperity, and a land where the powerful do not prey on the powerless," Lord Varys replied. "The powerful always prey on the powerless. That is how they became powerful in the first place," scoffed Tyrion. "Perhaps," said Lord Varys. "Or perhaps we have become so used to the horror, we assume there is no other way" (*Game of Thrones*, Season 5, Episode 1).

The above exchange between Lord Varys and Tyrion sums up one of the main assumptions of constructivist theory—the world in which we reside is socially constructed. This means there is a joint constructed understanding among individuals of the world and how it operates. This understanding forms the basis for shared assumptions about the world and how states should behave in it.

Just like realism and liberalism, constructivism makes several basic assumptions when explaining state behavior. Importantly, constructivism views the world from the lens of the individual level of analysis. This means individuals are the most important actors and, thus, the state cannot be treated as a unitary actor; rather, individual leaders and individuals in society as well as their preferences must be considered. For example, realism would argue the anarchical nature of the international system in Westeros-Essos led each region to seek power to protect itself. Thus, it does not matter if Robert Baratheon, Joffrey Baratheon, Ned Stark, Daenerys Targaryen, or Jon Snow sits upon the Iron Throne and is the most benevolent sovereign; each would behave the same way and seek power to ensure their survival.

From the constructivist perspective, though, the individual leader's preferences must be considered. Ned Stark and Jon Snow care more for their subjects than do Robert or Joffrey Baratheon. Daenerys' interests in power differ from those Jon Snow seeks or that of Little Finger, for example. As a result of these differences in preferences, the actions of the leaders and the way the state behaves will therefore also differ. This is because preferences are not based upon a simple left-right continuum as the previous theories of realism and liberalism suggest. The structure of the system, regardless of whether it is viewed as anarchic (neo-realism), made up of institutions (neo-liberalism), or social norms (constructivism), does not single-handedly determine the behavior of states. Rather, constructivism argues preferences form as a result of an amalgamation of variables interacting over time which influence the way states make rational calculations. In other words, actors start off with certain assumptions regarding the potential for the maximum possible outcome regarding their preferences. Over time, through interaction with other states, learning, institutions, the development of social norms, the formation of regimes, and as a result of the structure of the system and changing conceptions of relative and absolute power, etc., state preferences evolve (Wendt 1999).

In line with critical identity perspectives, constructivism argues actors in the system and the system itself are mutually constituted. In other words, both individuals and the environment in which they live have the potential to impact and, also, shape each other. There are weak and strong social constructs. Weak constructs are dependent on facts alone. Strong constructs, on the other hand, rely on human perception and the knowledge that forms the basis of norms in society. Individuals relate to each other through these constructs, or ideas. Constructivism is particu-

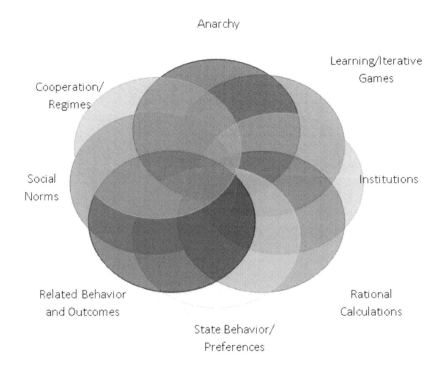

Figure 4.1. Formation of Preferences. *Source*: **Young 2019.**

larly concerned with how these ideas come to be and the implications they have on society (Sarason and Sarason 2009).

Not long after Jon Snow takes Ygritte prisoner, they begin to argue over who has the rightful claim to the lands in the North and north of the wall over which they fight. Ygritte argues, "They're not your lands. We've been here the whole time. You lot came along and just put up a big wall and said it was yours." Jon proclaims, "My father was Ned Stark. I have the blood of the First Men. My ancestors lived here same as yours." Jon's proclamation prompt Ygritte to ask, "So why're you fighting us?" to which, Jon has no reply (*Game of Thrones,* Season 2, Episode 7). This exchange is emblematic of the point constructivists, and Lord Varys, make about the world in which we live: Our perceptions of the world and why or how it functions are often constructed. If we can deconstruct these perceptions and focus on our similarities, we can begin to move past our differences, or those things that prevent us from cooperating.

"Northerners" and "Southerners" also have very different perceptions of each other and recognize differences in their cultures, such as dress and religion, for instance. These differences cause contention between those in the North and those in the South. In general, "Southerner" is a term used to describe those living south of the region known as The Neck. Northerners are, then, of course, those that live north of The Neck. The Wildlings, though, argue anyone south of the wall is a Southerner; even the people living in the kingdom of the North. The Andals, who conquered Westeros, imposed their religion and language on most of the continent. Though the Andals' influence did extend to the North, their ability to assimilate the people in the North to their culture was not as successful. In fact, the North is one of the few areas where the traditions of the First Men remain strong and they still practice the religion of the Old Gods of the Forest.

Another difference between Northerners and Southerners is the South's reverence for aristocracy and its adherence to a more class-based ranking of individuals where titles like "peasant," "noble," "knight," "lord," etc., matter. Nobility and knights are not common in Northern society, however. The North also is not known for lavish displays of wealth like seen in the noble courts in the South. In fact, upon his arrival in King's Landing, Eddard Stark scoffs at the ways of the South proclaiming, "They strut around like roosters . . . !" (*Game of Thrones,* Season 1, Episode 4).

Another example of the clash in cultures between the North and the South occurs during an exchange between Osha and Theon Greyjoy when she says, "I just don't understand how you Southerners do things." Interestingly, Theon responds, "I'm not a Southerner." To which Osha declares, "You're from south of the Wall. That makes you a 'Southerner' to me!" (*Game of Thrones,* Season 1, Episode 7). Craster says the same to Jon Snow (*Game of Thrones,* Season 2, Episode 1). This exchange is another example of how perceptions matter. To Southerners, anyone north of the Neck is a Northerner. To those beyond the wall, though, anyone south of it is a Southerner.

Ideas, identities, interests, institutions, and norms are all important when explaining the relationship between agency and structure as well as state behavior. Ideas are those things that give the world meaning whereas identities are the perception of oneself and the perception of others. Identities form the basis of interests which, in turn, help to shape individuals' preferences. Out of these preferences, or relatively stable set of identities and interests, form institutions which provide rules to guide behavior. Norms emerge as a result of institutions and help further the acceptance of ideas, identities, and interests.

There is general consensus among scholars that a norm can be defined "as a standard of appropriate behavior for actors within a given identity." Norms also contain a "prescriptive (or evaluate) quality of 'ought-ness' that sets [them] apart from other types of rules" (Finnemore and Sikkink 1998, 891). Appropriate behavior is determined by the "disapproval or stigma" associated with not adhering to the standard of appropriate behavior which has been established, and not as a result of the noncompliance with a legal rule. Moreover, a norm can be identified as being present when adherence to a particular type of behavior results in "praise, or in the case of a highly internalized norm," when the action "is so taken for granted that it provokes no reaction whatsoever" (Finnemore and Sikkink 1998, 892).

Norms become particularly important in the evolution of preferences since norms form the basis for the "collective expectations for the proper behavior of actors within a given identity" (Katzenstein 1996, 5). In other words, norms help regulate the behavior of states. In particular, "norms exert powerful influence on the shaping of state behavior, making actors understand what is acceptable in international society" (Shannon 2000, 295). The norms in question evolve and change, and these developments influence states to also adapt to the morphing environment of norms and their influence on state behavior. As a result, state behavior likewise evolves.

The interactions of states with all these intervening causal variables, as well as the development of regimes, and the interplay of cooperation, will result in different states placing different values on the same interest. Therefore, because of the myriad of different variables in the international system, preferences will be defined and shaped differently depending upon the amount of interaction and the order of interaction of states in the system (Shannon 2000). As a result, cooperation will occur for a variety of reasons, at different times, and at varying degrees. This suggests cooperation is not static over time as interest-based theories indicate. Moreover, cooperation is not determined merely by changing social norms. Rather, because at any given time states are impacted by a swirling set of factors varying in intensity and degree, cooperation becomes dynamic, changing as the rate of interaction changes over time.

What is most interesting about the perceived differences the Northerners and Southerners and Wildlings all have of each other, as discussed above, is that when the threat of the White Walkers grows, suddenly the differences no longer matter. After all, the White Walkers are more zombie-like than human-like and they seek to destroy all humans. The Northerners, Southerners, and Wildlings, all being human, begin to relate more with each other, than with the identity of the zombies. Thus, it is no longer about the North versus the South or the Wildlings versus the North, but the living verses the undead. As a result, the North, most of the South, and the Wildlings all band together to fight against the undead. Thus, as the variables change within the environment, so, too, will the identities, norms, and preferences of the state.

Since the international system is not explained by material interests, like power or economic prowess, but rather by perception and preferences, the international system can change. This is very different from the assumption of realism and liberalism which argues the international system is anarchic and that it is this anarchy which drives state behavior. As Alexander Wendt famously said, "Anarchy is what states make of it" (Wendt 1999, 56). For example, liberal institutionalism argues increased economic cooperation among states as well as the institution of rules to limit cheating and constrain state behavior will reduce the likelihood of war. Institutions like the League of Nations, NATO, or the UN are the key to enhancing stability. Constructivists argue, though, states behave the way they do because they are preprogrammed with the realist conception of state interaction and behavior. When states change their perspective and perception of the state of affairs, cooperation is possible. States cooperate when norms created by institutions shape their identity and preferences in such a way that cooperation seems optimal. Constructivists therefore challenge the logic of realism by arguing if the discourse or ideas and conceptions of states are changed, then state behavior and the relationships will change. In short, changing the way states and their leaders think about world politics will change the behavior of states and result in a more peaceful environment.

Though, realists argue all states seek power just as Tyrion argues, constructivists argue to suggest states deliberately seek outcomes that result in less than optimal results (because war is costlier than cooperation) is incorrect and a misinterpretation of the calculations states make regarding the perceived benefits from those outcomes. Over time, the understanding of what is in a state's self-interest and the weight given to a particular outcome by the state will change. Norms play a key role in constructivism's explanation of cooperation.

You will recall realism argues, according to the prisoner's dilemma, trust is not possible and therefore each state must defect and not cooperate in order to avoid the sucker's payoff. This lack of trust is why, when used to explain outcomes at the international level, conflict occurs. Liberalism, on the other hand, argues institutions can help overcome the anarchical nature of the international system by acting as a third-party mechanism that can facilitate trust. Critical identity perspectives, however, argue shared norms and values help states view each other as less threatening than states who share a different set of norms and values. Institutions help to create a shared set of norms which can then help reconstruct the way cooperation with another is viewed. Security communities, for example, form "whenever states become integrated to the point that they have a sense of community, which, in turn, creates the assurance that they will settle their differences short of war . . . creat[ing] not simply a stable order but . . . a stable peace" (Karl Deutsch as quoted in Adler and Barnett [1998, 3]). In other words, security communities are the result of an understanding of states that the use of violence is an unlikely resolution to disputes when conflict arises within the group.[1]

Research on security communities examines the role of social learning through norms, rules, and transactions which take place among actors in the international system. The understanding of these variables is important since they lead to the development of mutual trust among the members of the group. The growth of mutual trust is a necessary condition that enables individuals "to identify with those who were once on the other side of the cognitive divides . . . which, in turn, are the proximate necessary conditions for the development of dependent expectations of peaceful change." This is significant because "both mutual trust and collective identity . . . are the proximate necessary conditions for the development" of security communities (Adler and Barnett 1998, 45). In other words, over time as actors engage with each other through transactions, communications, and social exchanges, a process of social learning takes place that facilitates the development of knowledge regarding other actors' behaviors as well as the fostering of normative processes that lead to mutual trust and collective identity formation. Thus, it is not the structure of the system, but the convergence of expectations, behavior, and the formation of a collective identity that fosters peace.

Furthermore, as identity grows "states no longer rely on concrete international organizations to maintain trust but do so through knowledge and beliefs about the other." In addition, "identification of friend or foe" is possible as a result of "years of experiences and encounters that shapes the cultural definitions of threat" (Adler and Barnett 1998, 46). This identification helps actors to distinguish between those inside the boundaries of the community which in turn enhances the ability of the members to anticipate the behavior and action of other members in the group. Thus, in short, the settlement of disputes by some means other than war is explained as a result of the security communities that develop around the expectations of the members forged out of the mutual trust and collective identity that has formed.

We see examples of security communities in *Game of Thrones*. The North, for instance, calls upon several houses to aid in its defense on multiple occasions. When Lyanna Mormont refuses to show allegiance to Stannis Baratheon she firmly states, she "and Bear Island know no other king but the King in the North, whose name is Stark" (*Game of Thrones*, Season 5, Episode 2). This sentiment is shared among many vassals in the northern region who have long known the reign of the Starks over the North and have come to trust that it rules with honor and adheres to a sense of justice. Importantly, and representative of security communities, when a dispute arises within the region controlled by the North it is settled in a way that upholds justice, reducing the likelihood of conflict. For example, the North holds court allowing individuals to air their grievances, which it then attempts to rectify. Though considered different territories ruled by different houses, regions within the north of Westeros share a common culture (built around the Starks' sense of honor and justice) which they see as separating them from "Southerners" like those in King's Landing. This, too, makes it easier for Robb and, later, Jon to gain support in their quest to defend the North from the White Walkers and King's Landing.

In sum, constructivism argues perceptions matter. Importantly, perceptions can change over time as variables change. Thus, individuals, and states, can also change. This means, unlike realism that argues cooperation is unlikely because the self-interested nature of states makes trust difficult, or liberalism which argues institutions are necessary to help overcome the self-interested nature of states and lack of trust, constructivism argues it just depends on how the environment presents itself as to whether cooperation will occur.

Without the threat of the White Walkers, the North and the Wildlings would still be at war with each other. One might argue it is just a temporary alliance built to secure the survival of both sides. Constructivists, on the other hand, would point to Jon Snow giving several Wildlings leadership roles and his making them trusted advisors as evidence that perceptions about the threat posed to the other side have changed, or at the very least, are beginning to change. Either way, cooperation has, for now at least, been achieved in the Seven Kingdoms, even after the defeat of the White Walkers. Constructivists would argue this is because perceptions, identities, interests, norms, etc., have changed the preferences of individuals and helped forge a tentative security community.

MARXISM AND WORLD SYSTEMS THEORY

Marx agued history is really about the struggle of the classes, with each state in history representing another stage in the progression of class struggles where elites arrange society in order to ensure they remain on top. The focus of his theory involved a class-based analysis within the larger framework of the domestic/state level analysis. The proletariat (workers/common man) are locked into a system that prevents them from escaping the bottom class in society and entering the realm of the bourgeoisie (owners of the means of production/elites). In other words, the rich control everything and do what they can to make certain it stays that way. The proletariat are perceived as objects and not as equal beings by the bourgeoisie, who are the ones who control their destinies. The differences in class interests between the proletariat and the bourgeoisie intensifies as an industrialized economic system increases the economic divisions of the two classes. Ultimately, such divisions result in a class struggle or a form of social class revolution where the proletariat revolt against the bourgeoisie (Marx and Engles 1997, 13–25).

The bourgeoisie make certain the proletariat do not challenge the way the bourgeoisie have constructed society for fear they might lose the benefits they receive from the current construction. One of the tactics they employ to prevent any potential challenge is to alienate the worker, both from the means of production as well as from his fellow worker. Workers have no say in the goods they produce, nor do they have an ownership stake. As a result, workers are left with only their labor to sell. Marx views this as coerced, forced labor with the worker's production only increasing the wealth of the bourgeoisie and perpetuating the system that works against their interests and which results in the alienation they face.

In addition to alienation from the means of production, workers are also alienated from each other. According to Marx, this alienation is a result of the competitive labor market created by the bourgeoisie that pits worker against worker. Also, instead of workers participating in labor that is created by their own will, which Marx argues is part of our species-essence to do, workers are forced into labor in which they have no ownership. This ownership makes labor a means to an end and deprives the proletariat of a necessary aspect of social life. In total, alienation from the means of production is a tactic which keeps the worker locked into a system that prevents him from engaging not only in important tasks that enrich the worker, but also separates him from his fellow worker. Social capital, or the networks of people and individuals who live and work in a particular society, is not allowed to flourish as a result. This is important because social capital is a core variable needed for social revolutions to occur. By alienating the worker and limiting the growth of social capital, the bourgeoisie reduce the likelihood of revolution.

Marx also argues religion is a tool used by the bourgeoisie to control the proletariat. In fact, Marx famously refers to religion as the "opium of the people," (Marx and Engles 2008, 42), or, more commonly referred to as the "opiate of the masses." Similar to Max Weber's argument in *The Protestant Ethic and the Spirit of Capitalism*, Marx argued religion reduced the suffering of the people because it provided them with illusions of the rewards they would receive in the afterlife. These beliefs made the toils in which men and women faced under the system constructed by the bourgeoisie more tolerable. Further, it prevents individuals from even recognizing the class struggle and oppression they face since it is excused as earthly burdens one must face to reap the rewards after one's death. Thus, for Marx, religion acts as a tool to prevent the proletariat from questioning their fate and, thus, rising in revolution against the bourgeoisie.

Marx's interpretation of the development of human history differs from most theories in the realist and liberal paradigms that view the world from a top-down approach. In other words, the environment in which an individual resides dictates his or her behavior. Marx, though, believed "the degree of economic development attained by a given people or during a given epoch form the foundation upon which the state institutions . . . evolved" (Tucker 1978, 681). Importantly, how society is arranged and how the institutions are formed are a reflection of the "pervasive beliefs, values, stories, etc., of the dominant ruling group and class" (Parenti 2006, 12). In line with constructivism, Marx argues society is socially constructed, and done so in a way that benefits certain groups more so than others resulting in a class struggle.

The class struggle described by Marx mirrors that in *Game of Thrones*. The nobility controls society. They represent the top, albeit minority, group in society. The farmers, peasants, blacksmiths, etc., all live at the pleasure of the elites that rule over them. Social mobility is extremely limited, and the nobility socially construct society to make certain these standards are accepted and not challenged. In fact, there are only a few families in the series that dominate all of Westeros and Essos. They form alliances and maneuver themselves through marriage and other means to make certain their positions in society are not challenged. For example, marriage secures the Tyrell's their position within society and ensures their lineage continues uninterrupted. In addition, any sign of dissent is stamped out. For example, during the royal procession that takes place after Myrcella sails off for Dorne, Joffrey is jeered at by his starving subjects. When the crowd turns unruly, he orders his guards to execute them (*Game of Thrones*, Season 2, Episode 6).

World systems theory uses the systemic level of analysis to apply Marx's domestic-class–based-assumptions to state behavior at the international level. Specifically, world systems theory argues the world system is made up of three structural constants which are essential, without which no fundamental transformation of the world system can occur (Boswell and Chase-Dunn 2000). These structural elements are made up of the capitalist world economy, an interstate system, and a core-periphery hierarchy.

Capitalism is "the accumulation of resources by means of exploitation in the production and sale of commodities for profit" (Boswell and Chase-Dunn 2000, 20). Within the capitalist world economy two types of exploitation exist—primary exploitation and secondary exploitation. Primary exploitation occurs between labor and the owners of the means of production whereas secondary exploitation occurs between the "capital-rich and the capital-poor" with each type of exploitation involving the use of coercive power for the accumulation of capital (Boswell and Chase-Dunn 2000, 21). Applied to the systemic level, this view regards how the division of labor based on capitalism involves an occupational and geographical division in the world-system. States which can legitimize the exploitation of the labor of other sates "receive a larger share of the surplus," whereas the states that are exploited remain in their disadvantaged situation (Wallerstein 1974, 349). Labor here related to states is a commodity, a tradable good, that can be sold to the international market, which is controlled by the states that have the means.

The importance of the interstate system regarding the development of the world system involves the changing of the interstate system regarding the world polity and the world order. A world polity is made up of shared values and norms which are enforced through international organizations. These values and norms do not necessarily have to coincide with economic or geopolitical interests but may involve cultural and epistemological concerns. A world order, on the other hand, is concerned with geopolitical and economic interests. Cultural concerns and enforcement by international organizations matter much less. "Most important for world-system theory is that a change in a world polity *transforms* the definition of a system's logic and goals, while a change in world orders is a better or worse achievement of preexisting common goals" (Boswell and Chase-Dunn, 2000, 25).

Finally, the core-periphery hierarchy is a direct result of the capitalist world economy and the interstate system and reflects dimensions of power, dependency, and productivity. The core-periphery hierarchy is made up of three levels. Dominant states, or those states with advanced technological abilities and highly skilled labor forces, are found in the core. Core states completely dominate the world economy by extracting raw materials from weaker states and engaging in capital-intensive production. The weakest states, or those states engaged in primarily agricultural and labor-intensive activities, are found in the periphery. The states located in the semiperiphery are more stable politically and economically than the periphery zones and are only dependent upon the core. These states do have the possibility to mobilize their status over time, and in fact some semiperiphery states were part of the "peripheral areas" that later evolved to a semiperiphery status due to the "changing geopolitics of an expanding world economy" (Wallerstein 1974, 349). States within the periphery on the other hand are both politically and economically highly dependent upon those states found in the core or the semiperiphery. Their ability to mobilize their status over time is much more limited.

Similar to Marx's theory, world systems theory argues that core states create an international order benefiting them while locking the periphery into a position that keeps them from joining the core or revolting (Wallerstein 1974). Since countries are part of a world economic system, which happens to be capitalist, the same division of labor, alienation, and exploitation Marx describes takes place between the core and periphery. As a result, an unequal distribution of rewards and resources occurs, just as it occurs in domestic society. This unequal cycle just as, according to Marx, the worker is locked into his plight from which the system prevents him from escaping.

Though religion is not a focus of world systems theory, core states, nevertheless, construct institutions to help shape the beliefs of individual states. The United Nations, for example, is viewed by liberalism as an organization constructed to promote peace and help spread values associated with such. However, world systems theorists argue international institutions, like the United Nations, are constructed by the most dominant states in order to perpetuate a world order that greatly favors them. The same is true for organizations like the International Monetary Fund (IMF) and World Bank. For example, countries that need loans from these organizations are required to follow certain guidelines set forth by the organizations that often require the restructuring of their economy to align with "standards" set forth by the Ricardo model of comparative advantage (McDonald 2018). Often, periphery countries find it difficult to compete with core countires like the United States and see their economy become less diversified and more dependent upon the core, just as Marx argues happens to the worker. In short, the core states who created these organizations made certain to do so in a way that benefited them at the expense of the periphery while making certain the periphery is unable to break free from the constructed system.

Since Westeros-Essos is devoid of a lot of international institutions there are not many examples similar to the UN. The Iron Bank, however, is similar to the IMF and World Bank rolled into one. The Iron Bank is a financial institution that lends money to countries in need. The Iron Bank is the most powerful banking institution in Westeros-Essos and is arguable the most powerful entity as well since it is responsible for the funding of wars. Though there are few restrictions placed on countries that borrow money from the Iron Bank like there are when it comes to dealings with the IMF or World Bank, one requirement is that you pay your debt back to the bank. If you do not pay your debt, the Iron Bank is known to fund wars against you. Thus, the Iron Bank is more than just an independent financial institution; it is a political one as well. The IMF and World Bank are criticized for also being political and for constructing a system that benefits some over others.

In sum, Marxism and world systems theory view the world as socially constructed, but specifically constructed by a certain group of individuals/states to benefit them at the expense of others. Those that are exploited (the proletariat or periphery) are locked in a system that is difficult from which to break free. Elites in society find ways to reinforce the social construction of society so that those whom they exploit either do not question their fate or find themselves in a position (either through alienation or otherwise) unable to demand more equitable treatment. Thus, it is not about a struggle for power or a lack of rule of law or democratic institutions. Rather, the way the world operates is a result of how it was socially constructed by a group of fortunate individuals/states that found themselves in a position to structure the world in a way that benefits some over others.

FEMINISM

In her book, *Gendering World Politics,* Ann Tickner suggests to successfully incorporate gender, and to a greater extent feminist theory, in international relations, theories must expand beyond the traditional realist and liberal approaches and incorporate elements of social construction of meaning, historical variability, as well as examine hidden power relations. This expansion serves to reveal the hidden gender attributes already present, and often ignored, in international relations theory. As a result, because reflectivists are concerned with ideas that shape the world as well as "understanding how we think about the world," feminists tend to identify specifically with this sector of the third debate—even though the inclusion of gender by scholars outside of the feminist realm has been lacking (Tickner 2001, 25). Specifically, normative theory, historical sociology, critical theory, and postmodernism, according to Tickner, have provided the space feminists need to incorporate elements of gender into the traditional international relations debate because of their focus on social construction and the historical development of society.

To that end, feminists argue that the traditional realist perspective of security and the state should be expanded to go beyond its historically masculine characteristics to incorporate gendered identities as well as to include such things as threats to social, environmental and economic well-being. Doing so allows for a better understanding of a state and its security interests because it incorporates "issues of identity within their social context" (Tickner 2001, 46). In other words, this bottom-up approach provides a better understanding of contemporary insecurities as well as the way "people are responding to these insecurities by reworking their understanding of how their own predicament fits into broader structures of violence and oppression" that go beyond the basic realist top-down premise of military threat and insecurity that is consistently centered on the state (Tickner 2001, 46–48).

Moreover, by examining the culture and identity of states regarding their security-seeking behavior, feminists can construct a more comprehensive definition of security that includes more than just the realist definition centered on hegemonic aspirations and self-interested behavior. Feminists argue by limiting states' national security interests to such masculine characteristics "privileges certain types of behavior over others" constraining the options states have when establishing policies regarding national security (Tickner 2001, 48–53). For instance, when discussing the realist argument regarding the security dilemma, feminists suggest the parable of man's amoral, self-interested behavior in the state of nature is nothing more than a male characteristic that has been socially constructed over time. In addition, strong leaders have become synonymous with having typical male-dominate traits like strength, power, sternness, fearlessness, and unwillingness to compromise. In order to be seen as a strong leader, thus, females must adopt these male characteristics. This creates a paradox, though, because women who have demonstrated these male-dominant traits are also seen as more unlikable.

Brienne of Tarth is considered a very powerful swordsmith, though because of her stature and more hardened facial features, she is considered very masculine. If a man, her power and exemplary skills with a sword would win her much praise. Instead, she is often jeered at. "All my life men like you have sneered at me," she once said to Jamie Lannister, "and all my life I've been knocking men like you into the dust" (*Game of Thrones*, Season 2, Episode 8). Hillary Clinton's political history has been similar. Once ridiculed for not wearing enough makeup when her husband was running for governor of Arkansas, Hillary has faced continuous criticism for not being feminine enough yet backlash for being too weak when she has shown signs of emotion. Chile's first female president Michelle Bachelet noted that female leaders are held to a different standard, one that even includes evaluations of clothing, appearances of the physique, and how they interact in public (La Tercera 2017). To overcome such gendered classifications which are prevalent globally, India's first female prime minister Indira Gandhi purposefully sought to frame her political identity with the nation, with the slogan of India is Indira. The identification of the nation-state with her persona helped blur the gendered identity, although Indira also benefited from taking on a metaphoric representation as the mother of India in her political campaign (Barua 1996, 228).

An important point feminism makes about the ability of states to cooperate has to do with the way we socially construct the characteristic of leaders. If the world is made up of leaders, the majority of whom are men that have these more aggressive characteristics or females that have adopted these characteristics, then is it really all that surprising there is a lack of cooperation and so much war in the international system? This is not to suggest that a world full of female leaders would make the world more peaceful. As Madeline Albright once famously said, "I'm not a person who thinks the world would be entirely different if it was run by women. If you think that, you've forgotten what high school was like." However, if we reconstruct what it means to be a good leader, including those more "female" characteristics, like empathy, emotion, and diplomacy, then, perhaps, cooperation would be more possible.

Daenerys' rise to power is a good example of how a powerful leader is typically perceived and the way that perception can change over time. When Daenerys first comes to power she exhibits several typical characteristics of a male leader. Those that she feels can help her cause, like the unsullied, for example, she treats justly. Others who threaten her power, or who do not uphold the values she does, she ruthlessly kills; the nailing of the masters to the posts in Meereen is a good example (*Game of Thrones*, Season 4, Episode 4). Her advisors suggest, though, a more conciliatory approach might produce better results. When Meereen is under attack from the Maseters' fleet, Daenerys decides to resolve the conflict by increasing her military strength and "returning [the Masters'] cities to the dirt." Tyrion implores her to use diplomacy instead, begging her not to become like her father. It is important to note, diplomacy does not mean that power cannot be exerted. Successful negotiations, recall, require one to "speak softly but carry a big stick. To that end, Daenerys agrees to meet with the Masters and discuss terms to end the war. When the Masters do not agree to Daenerys' terms, she increases her bargaining leverage by using her dragon to destroy all of the Masters' ships (Season 6, Episode 9).

Though force was still used in the end, the fact she was willing to negotiate and not just immediately react by waging war shows growth on her part as a leader. She also declares she will answer injustice with justice, showing signs of compassion not typical with the Dothraki leaders before her, or most of the main leaders in *Game of Thrones* for that matter, except perhaps the Starks. Finally, she is more likely than most to listen to the advice of her advisors and show compassion and appreciation for those beneath her, like the Unsullied for example. Compassion, empathy, and a willingness to compromise are not always associated with strong leaders, yet, Daenerys exhibits these characteristics, while no doubt still showing herself as a capable leader.

Although there are many different branches of feminism, all feminists agree gender must be incorporated into the traditional approaches in the study of international relations if equality among all people is to be achieved. This goes beyond simply establishing norms and institutions that acknowledge the inequality gap between men and women, but by also acknowledging that the way in which we think about the world must be changed in order to recognize the masculine, patriarchic, state-centered outlook used to view, understand, explain, and predict state behavior, relationships, and interactions at the local, national, and global level. This includes the disparity that not only exists between the traditional masculine/feminine debate, but also the erroneous distinction between the North/South divide which imposes Western ideals on the third world and which assumes a common relationship and characteristics between the identities of the two regions. Without recognizing the importance of gender, the plight of women and minorities will never be fully rectified.

Though at first *Game of Thrones* does not seem like it would be a good champion for feminism, the show promotes the principles of feminism quite well. If you think about it, the show is full of women rising to power and overcoming and exacting revenge on the men who have treated them unfairly. Sansa Stark gets her revenge on Ramsay Bolton, assuming the role as Head of Winterfell in Jon's absence. Daenerys, who is treated cruelly by her brother, Viserys Targaryen, who thinks he is destined to be the leader of the Seven Kingdoms, meets his demise as Daenerys silently watches, marking the start of her rise to power. Joffrey, who has a particularly cruel side when it comes to women, meets his untimely demise at the hands of a woman, Lady Olenna Tyrell, through the use of a "woman's weapon," or poison. These are just a few of the many examples. In addition, we begin to see an evolving understanding of what it means to be a good leader. Daenerys, as explained above, has begun to show more "female" traits, and Jon Snow also demonstrates traits of empathy, compassion, and a willingness to engage in diplomacy, thus highlighting one of the main arguments feminism makes about the benefits reconstructing the way we view the world and those who lead it can have with regard to producing more cooperate outcomes.

	Constructivism	Marxism/World Systems Theory	Feminism
Major Actors	Individual, Collective Identities	Individual, Collective Identities	Individual, Collective Identities
Human Nature	Blank slate shaped by environment	Blank slate shaped by environment	Blank slate shaped by environment
State	Reflection of beliefs, norms, ideas, and identities	Reflection of beliefs, norms, ideas, and identities	Reflection of beliefs, norms, ideas, and identities
International System	Anarchy is what states make of it	Socially constructed by elites in society	Socially constructed by elites in society

Figure 4.2. Critical Identity Perspectives. *Source:* **Young 2019.**

CONCLUSION

Though critical identity theories vary regarding what they seek to explain and the ways in which they examine international relations, all are similar in that they view the role of ideas, interests, institutions, perceptions, and the way these influence our social construction of the world in which we live as being particularly important in explaining state behavior. This theory is much more flexible when it comes to making predictions about the world and explaining state behavior. Because it views variables as ever-changing and not fixed over time, though, it makes it much more difficult as a theory within which to work compared to say, realism, which relies on only a few variables which remain static over time. Nevertheless, critical identity perspectives add a layer of understanding that realism and liberalism miss, opening the prospect for more cooperation than the two other theories might suggest.

NOTES

1. The most common type of security communities are pluralistic communities. These communities "retain the legal independence of separate governments, but possess a compatibility of core values derived from common institutions, and mutual responsiveness—a matter of mutual identity and loyalty, a sense of we-ness, and are integrated to the point that they entertain dependable expectations of peaceful change" (Adler and Barnett 1998, 7).

FIVE

Human Rights

Our daily lives are embedded with recurrent themes of challenges and defenses of human rights. The solitary confinement of a prisoner, the denial of the right to assembly of a group of peaceful protesters, the sex trafficking of women across various states, and the practice of the death penalty, are various examples of what today constitutes a violation of human rights. Responses to defend human rights, such as campaigns to end torture and ill-treatment and nongovernmental organizations that work to raise awareness of women's rights issues are different means through which individuals and groups have strived to defend human rights. This chapter offers an overview of the modern developments of human rights, including the dissemination of the legal frameworks of human rights in the periods following the great wars of the twentieth century. Using some of the examples of the legal standards, the chapter provides an in-depth examination of human rights related to torture, ill-treatment, and women's rights, and how it may be used to analyze the plot and character developments in *Game of Thrones*.

MODERN DEVELOPMENTS OF HUMAN RIGHTS

The changes to the international system following the end of the Second World War (1939–1945) influenced the development of modern conceptions of human rights and the expansion of international legal mechanisms to enforce human rights at the international and domestic levels. Human rights are a set of "moral rights of the highest order" (Donnelly 2013, 11), one which defines a broad guideline as to what ought to be protected for all individuals. They empower citizens to "vindicate their rights, to insist that these standards be realized" (Donnelly 2013, 12) by all political actors. The context of the Second World War, with grave human rights atrocities documented in the extermination of the Jewish population in Europe and the abuses against civilians and prisoners of war throughout East Asia, provided impetus for the international community to develop an expansive set of standards to safeguard individuals' human rights.[1] The Nuremburg War Crime Trials (1945–1946) and the International Military Tribunal for the Far East, or the Tokyo Trials, (1946–1948) were the first two international tribunals that prosecuted and punished individual war criminals. They established the foundations for modern justice on human rights by prosecuting and punishing leaders of Nazi Germany and Japan for "crimes against peace and against humanity" (Overy 2003, 1–2; Futamura 2008). These precedents had a durable effect in setting new guidelines of international conduct on what ought to proceed when in fact grave human rights violations are committed during armed conflict. Future international tribunals, such as the Yugoslavian (ICTY; 1993–2017) and Rwandan Tribunals (ICTR; 1994–2015) expanded the scope of crimes against humanity tied to an armed conflict as noted in the Nuremberg and Tokyo Tribunals. The ICTY tried those responsible for war crimes such as the 1995 Srebrenica genocide of 8,000 Bosnian Muslim men and boys by Serb forces during the Balkans conflict in the 1990s and the ICTR attempted to bring to justice those who had contributed to orchestrating the gravest crimes of genocide in Rwanda in 1994.

Despite their advances in bringing justice, both tribunals were criticized for their excessive spending and for falling short of indicting and convicting all the senior government personnel responsible for the crimes (e.g., 2013 ICTR's appeal judges' ruling that threw out convictions against Justin Mugenzi and Prosper Mugiraneza in 2011). Nonetheless, as these tribunals provided a means through which criminal accountability could still be independently administered for a state whose national jurisdiction had disintegrated, they set a precedent of accountability for other states in similar conditions of conflict. Both tribunals' opinions concluded that crimes against humanity can exist as "self-standing crimes," even in the "absence of armed conflict" (Clapham 2003, 43).

As the Nuremburg and the Tokyo Trials unfolded, human rights rose to the center of international politics with the proliferation of legal instruments. These included the founding documents of the United Nations (UN), the intergovernmental organization that was created to prevent another war and mediate international crises by providing a forum for discussion among states. The first of these documents was the UN Charter, drafted and signed in the San Francisco meeting on June 26, 1945. The Preamble of the Charter set forth the organization's goal as promoting the fundamental human rights of all men and women, in addition to the renunciation of war, the promotion of peace, and a standard of protection of individuals' human rights (United Nations 2018a).

The Universal Declaration of Human Rights (UDHR),[2] adopted three years later in 1948, further defined a comprehensive set of internationally recognized individual human rights. At times referred to as the "International Magna Carta," the Preamble of the UDHR recognized the "equal and inalienable rights of all members of the human family" as being based on the "foundation of freedom, justice, and peace in the world" (United Nations 2018b). The Declaration established a "standard of decent social and governmental practice" (Nickel 1987, 4). With a total of thirty articles, the Declaration extrapolated on each individual human being's rights, specifying for instance a person's right to life (Article 3), right not to be held in slavery or servitude (Article 4), right to not be subject to torture or to cruel, inhuman or degrading punishment (Article 5), rights related to working hours (Article 24), and rights of adequate standards of living (Article 25), among other things (United Nations 2018b). These rights cover a range of economic, social, political, and even psychological treatment matters and helped further define human rights. Based on these measures, human rights norms could now be understood as "social and legal standards that specify how moral beliefs rooted in Western liberal conception of universal human dignity, as articulated in the UN's 1948 Universal Declaration of Human Rights, should direct behavior" (Clark 2001, 11).

Along with the specification of what constituted fundamental human rights, the Declaration was symbolically important in setting a universal rule of conduct for all people. The Universal Declaration of Human Rights was a nonbinding resolution of the United Nations General Assembly (GA). However, it was designed to set a standard, a first step, toward other binding agreements. And while it was a nonbinding document, given its role as one of the founding documents of human rights, it could not always fit into the legal categorization of whether the document was binding or nonbinding. Scholars assert that the Declaration is "binding on all states as customary international law through state practice and *opinion juris*" (Shelton 2000, 449).[3]

Customary international law is understood as a set of international obligations, which are shared and established through consistent international practices across civilized nations. As one of the "two main sources of international legal obligation" customary law "requires compliance" from states (Shelton 2000, 1). The UDHR is considered to be a source of customary international law, and thus, the human rights principals it enshrines are binding international legal obligations upon states. Such ideas are reaffirmed in the *Filartiga v. Pena-Irala* case, when the United States Court of Appeals for the Second Circuit referred to the resolution for the Universal Declaration of Human Rights in concluding that torture was prohibited under international law (Uniset 1980). This case adds legal weight to the UDHR which had originally begun from a nonbinding UN GA Resolution. In part, it supports the argument that the existence of the rights alone, as noted in the UDHR, could act as a backdrop for citizens of individual states to question their states' behaviors when it falls short of respecting these universally accepted rights. This position has been explored by scholars who examine the effects of international treaty ratification on states' behavior. According to Simmons, treaties can constrain states' behavior because they define the "expectations gap when governments fail to live up to their provisions" (Simmons 2009, 14). The gap that is felt by voters when states do not adhere to treaty standards can affect a regime's political future. Relating these ideas to human rights, treaty norms facilitate transnational advocacy work on holding states accountable for violating human rights.

The expansion of human rights from the UN Charter and the UDHR were complemented with additional international legal instruments that recognized and asserted more rights for individuals. Scholars classify this proliferation of human rights from new treaties as part of the emergence of three generations of human rights. Each generation of human rights standards complements the others' established principles (Lopes and Quénivet 2008, 206; Arat 2006). They are not exclusive and separate, and their status relies on the proper realization of each generation of human rights. Some scholars characterize the generations as forming before the end of the Second World War, during the waves of political changes as early as the French Revolution period (Vasak 1984). Specifically, they note the three principles of the French Revolution—*liberté*, *égalité*, and *fraternité* (liberty, equality, and fraternity) and their relevance to human rights. For instance, *liberté* corresponds to rights of freedom of expression of the people, *égalité* is embedded with ideas of improvement of social and economic rights, and *fraternité* relates to the premise of solidarity toward the amelioration of all individuals' human rights from the French Revolution (Vasak 1984). While the emergence of the rights related to the civic and political side may well have started during the French Revolution, the legal expression of these sets of human rights in international frameworks only developed in the latter periods with the adoption of the International Covenant on Civil and Political Rights in 1966 (ICCPR). Hence, given this context, there is merit to understanding the chronology of the generations of human rights along with the new treaties' developments as following the periods of the UN Charter and the UDHR.

The first-generation of rights, often referred to as the blue rights, embraces the rights of "security, property, and political participation" (Lopes and Quénivet 2008, 206) and has been mainly represented in the ICCPR. The ICCPR incorporated rights noted in the UDHR and made them legally binding. Under Article 28 of the ICCPR, the Human Rights Committee monitors the treaty obligations of states, examining state reports related to their compliance with the ICCPR. The rights that are monitored by the Human Rights Committee include the protection of life, liberty, and security of the person, and rights that overlap the political and legal, such as the right to a fair trial, as noted under Article 14 of the ICCPR (OHCHR 1966).

The second-generation rights, the red rights, include socioeconomic rights, such as the "right to welfare, education, and leisure" (Lopes and Quénivet 2008, 206). Many of these rights are referenced in the International Covenant on Economic, Social, and Cultural Rights ([ICESCR] 1966) under Article 13 (education), Article 4 (welfare), and Article 7 (leisure). The ICESCR is also legally binding. Under Article 2 of the ICESCR, states party to the covenant are to "take steps . . . to the maximum of its available resources," including legislative changes, to fully achieve the "realization of the rights" recognized by the covenant (OHCHR 1966).

Lastly, the third-generation rights or green rights are composed of "collective rights" (Lopes and Quénivet 2008, 206). These rights prioritize solidarity and the rights of a collective group. The Convention on the Elimination of all Forms of Discrimination Against Women ([CEDAW] 1979) and the Convention on the Rights of the Child (1989) are some of the examples of treaties that recognize the rights of a group of people that needs protection. A total of seven core international treaties are often identified along with the three generations of rights and they focus on specific human rights offenses and the discussion of rights focused on vulnerable populations. The totalities of the treaties include the Convention on the Prevention and Punishment of the Crime of Genocide (1948), International Convention on the Elimination of All Forms of Racial Discrimination ([ICERD] 1965), ICESCR, ICCPR, CEDAW, Convention against Torture and Other Cruel, Inhuman or Degrading Treatment or Punishment ([CAT] 1984), and the Convention on the Rights of the Child (Brysk and Jimenez 2012, 5). These conventions are all legally binding.

Along with these seven international legal standards, specific regions of the world also adopted their own human rights treaties to enforce rights. These included the European Convention on Human Rights, created within the Council of Europe in 1950; the American Convention on Human Rights adopted by the Organization of American States (OAS) in 1969; and the African Charter on Human and Peoples' Rights which entered into force in 1981 by party states to the Organization of African Unity. The rights in these conventions and charters mirrored many of the rights from the UDHR, apart from the absence of economic and social rights in the European Convention. Each document described a unique set of organs within each system that worked to preserve and promote human rights, such as the European Court of Human Rights (ECtHR), Inter-American Court of Human Rights (IACtHR) and the Inter-American Commission on Human Rights (IACHR), and the African Commission on Human and People's Rights.

The specialized organs such as the IACHR play an important role as the intermediary between the state in violation of human rights and the individuals from member states of the OAS petitioning their cases to be investigated by the commission. The petition requests are made by individual citizens who allege that a violation of human rights that challenge the existing treaties of the OAS have been made by the state against the individual. The IACtHR complements the work of the IACHR in producing advisory opinions, rulings, and recommendations on each case, the majority of which are against individual member states. As states within each region are party to the existing core international treaties in addition to regional conventions, there is an extra layer of oversight on these states to adhere to and respect human rights.

The progression of international mechanisms throughout the three generations reflected a fundamental shift in the international system as states voluntarily committed to human rights standards that could be legally enforced. In other words, while states maintained their structure as sovereign nations within their territorial boundaries, they were no longer immune from legal responsibility. By becoming party states to the treaties, states committed to a set of normative obligations and in doing so, added weight to the scope of human rights to be respected and observed by states.

The television series *Game of Thrones* is set in a different context and time period, where the absence of international treaty mechanisms is apparent. This may be a point of criticism by some who may view the application of contemporary human rights standards in connection with the series as a problem. However, if one understands how the horrible, scandalous, and revolting events in the series may mirror some of the past human rights abuses existent in our political history (e.g., Thirty Year War, the Holocaust, Rwandan Genocide, and the Nanjing Massacre), and how these moments were influential in the development of the modern human rights treaty system, there is a point to be made in studying the series in connection with human rights norms. There may be parallels to draw on from the series and our political environment, as human rights violations, despite their prevalence, are frowned upon in the series and the notion of a higher moral right, whether it be in civic, political, economic, social, or cultural form is present in each of the character's stories that involve power struggles and strategic calculations of each political actor's interests.

This chapter examines two human rights treaties, namely CAT and CEDAW, and applies them as normative measures to analyze *Game of Thrones*. Although there are other important treaties that are equally as applicable in the series such as the Convention on the Rights of the Child, CAT covers a broader set of violations, of which one can include the violations that also relate to children and other populations in terms of ill-treatment and torture. CEDAW is also examined, as the human rights violations against women are omnipresent in the series. In the sections to follow, we discuss these conventions more in depth, specify some of the human rights norms of importance, and then provide examples as to how each has been challenged on multiple occasions by the series.

CONVENTION AGAINST TORTURE (CAT)

The CAT advanced the ideas set forth under Article 5 of the Universal Declaration of Human Rights that prohibited torture. It established an aspect of enforcement for the prohibition of torture in a convention that was legally binding for states. International nongovernmental organizations such as Amnesty International were influential in bringing about the creation of the norm against torture with the 1972 Campaign for the Abolition of Torture and the development of the convention which entered into force in 1987 (Clark 2001). Under Article 1 of the convention, torture is defined as an "act by which severe pain or suffering whether physical or mental, is intentionally inflicted on a person" to obtain confessions or third-party information, including punishment for an act the individual is suspected of having committed (OHCHR 1987). This act must be deliberately committed by someone who is either a public official or is acting under the auspices of the state. Hence, if the act were committed by an individual with no affiliation to the state then the act would not constitute "torture" according to the CAT. In addition to ratifying the convention, states party to the document are expected to take measures to prohibit, suppress, and discourage torture via legislative, judicial, administrative changes and codify torture as an offense under its criminal law.

CAT lists a range of preventative obligations from the state to prevent torture and ill-treatment. One of such is the prohibition of *refoulement* (Article 3) or the non-return or extradition of a person to another state "where there are substantial grounds for believing that he would be in danger of being subjected to torture" (Weissbrodt and Hörtreiter 1999, 4). Forced return not only applies to a direct return but also an "indirect transfer to a third country" from where the individual may be returned to the state where "s/he would be in danger of being subjected to torture" (Weissbrodt and Hörtreiter 1999, 8). Non-*refoulement* provisions are listed under various other legal instruments (e.g., Convention on Refugees [1951]), although the specific reasoning related to the prevention of torture and nonforced return of an individual is only included in the CAT.

Another provision from the CAT refers to the education of law enforcement personnel who may be involved in "interrogation or treatment of any individual subjected to any form of arrest, detention, or imprisonment" (Article 10). This is a preventative measure to ensure the compliance of the state, along with the state personnel, of not conducting torture during interrogations as set forth in the convention.

Related to the convention, other international documents and legal interpretations further define the constitutive elements of torture and other cruel, inhuman, or degrading treatment of punishment. Specifically, on detainees and prisoners the GA Resolution 68/156 (A/RES/68/156 [2013]) notes that "solitary confinement" which is a condition of detention that deprives persons of their liberty and human rights may "amount to torture or other cruel, inhuman, or degrading treatment or punishment" (2013).

Other contexts where torture and ill-treatment may be present are described in the reports of UN Special Rapporteurs on Torture and Other Cruel, Inhuman or Degrading Treatment or Punishment. Rapporteurs are special envoys that monitor all states' record of torture and ill-treatment regardless of their party status to the CAT. In the 1986 Report from the Special Rapporteur Kooijmans, he notes that conditions of detention where the "rights of detainees" have been put aside, such as being exposed to beating, burning, extraction of nails, electric shocks, suspension, suffocation, sexual aggression, and exposure to excessive light or noise all constitute torture and ill-treatment (Kooijmans 1986, 28–29). Additionally, "any threats to kill or torture relatives and simulated executions" constitute torture (Kooijmans 1986, 29).

Such ideas are reiterated in the legal opinions issued by the UN Office of the High Commissioner of Human Rights (OHCHR). According to the OHCHR, for an act to be considered as torture or cruel, inhuman, and degrading treatment it ought to be intended for "intimidation and coercion" and for "punishment" (OHCHR 2011, 4). Similar arguments are made by the UN Voluntary Fund for Victims of Torture which elaborates further on the aspect of psychological torture of detainees. Interrogation techniques that involve threats to kill relatives as noted by the Special Rapporteur Kooijmans, in addition to "methods involving sexual humiliation, waterboarding, short shackling and using dogs to induce fear" all constitute torture or cruel, inhuman, or degrading treatment (OHCHR 2011, 23). These are just a few of the examples of torture and ill-treatment, which can be quite expansive.

As previously noted, the setting of *Game of Thrones* is a feudal system with dragons, witches, and enlightened beings clearly present different circumstances where international legal frameworks on human rights were absent. Nonetheless, there are ample cases of torture and ill-treatment in the television series that can be traced back to the ideas and human rights norms set forth in the CAT. Throughout the eight seasons of the series from 2011 to 2019, there were numerous noteworthy examples of the violation of torture, as defined by the CAT. These instances were in violation of Article 1 that defines torture and ill-treatment and its related standards of treatment of prisoners and detainees, torture as a way of punishing a third person(s), and Article 10 on the education of personnel involved in interrogations.

The earliest instance of torture was during Season 2, Episode 4 by King Joffrey Baratheon against his fiancée Sansa Stark. At the time, Sansa Stark's family was involved in the War of the Five Kings which followed after the execution of Sansa's father, Lord Eddard Stark of Winterfell by King Joffrey. Almost in a state of captivity, Sansa Stark is brought into the King's Court by King Joffrey to face punishment for her brother Robb Stark's victories in battle against King Joffrey's armies. Sansa is undressed forcefully, beaten, and is threatened to death with a sword by King Joffrey's men. These acts are done with the purpose to inflict both physical and mental pain on Sansa, as she faces the situation in the presence of other noblemen and women.

The definition of torture according to Article 1 of the convention identifies the act as purposeful and intentional with the aim to inflict psychological and physical or mental pain. Given these characteristics, Sansa's suffering constitutes a form of torture. Moreover, Sansa is threatened to death with the sword and the situation is only stopped when King Joffrey's uncle Tyrion Lannister intervenes. The threat of death intended for "punishment" and "intimidation" are forms of ill-treatment and torture as noted by the legal interpretations of the OHCHR (OHCHR 2011).

Other cases of torture and ill-treatment are related to the treatment of detainees and prisoners. During Season 2, Episode 4, peasants are brought in as prisoners to the Harrenhal Castle in Westeros and subjected to rigorous levels of interrogation. A prisoner is brought out every day for questioning, and after enduring a few beatings is strapped to a chair. Rats that have been trained to feed on flesh are put inside a wooden bucket which is tied to the prisoner's chest in the interrogation chair. Then, a torch of fire is used to push the rat closer to the chest of the prisoner with the eventual goal of making the rat eat away through the heart. This process is repeated on two occasions in the episode. Beatings, any form of usage of fire to cause burns, threat of death, and strapping of the individual to a chair are acts of torture and ill-treatment as specified by the 1986 Report from the Special Rapporteur on CAT Kooijmans and the legal interpretations from the OHCHR (OHCHR 2011; Kooijmans 1986).

Similar forms of torture against prisoners are also present in Episodes 2 and 6 of Season 3. Prince Theon Greyjoy, the heir of Lord Balon Greyjoy of the Iron Islands, is captured as a prisoner of war by the House of Bolton. He is held in solitary confinement and his body is suspended on a wooden cross and beaten by the guards. Although Theon seems to answer most of the questions asked of him by the interrogators, who include Lord Ramsay Bolton, the bastard son of Roose Bolton, his fingers are pierced with a spear, one of his fingers is cut off, nails are screwed inside his feet, and he is deprived of basic necessities, including water. The reasoning for the torture is not only for political motivations of extraction of information, but to render Theon psychologically impotent to the extent that he becomes a servant of Ramsay. According to Article 1 of the CAT, such acts constitute torture if it is intentionally inflicted to cause physical or mental harm by someone who is either a public official or with the consent of the state. In this case, Ramsay Bolton is the Lord of the House of Bolton where Theon has been taken as a prisoner of war, and the torture is purposeful with the aim to harm the prisoner. Furthermore, solitary confinement, which deprives the person their liberty and human rights, and the beating, extraction of nails, suspension, and denial of access to basic necessities are considered as torture and ill-treatment by the UN Special Rapporteur's 1986 Report and the legal interpretations of the OHCHR (Kooijmans 1986; OHCHR 2011).

A third case of torture involving a child overlaps with CAT and other international documents of human rights, namely the Convention on the Rights of the Child. King Stannis Baratheon is the Lord of Dragonstone who went to war against the Lannisters, the family of King Joffrey. His military camps are raided in the middle of the night, depleting his men of food supplies and heavy siege weapons. Relying on the advice of a witch Melissandre who sees visions of the future, Stannis and his wife Selyse decide that they have to sacrifice his daughter Princess Shireen of House Baratheon to win the next war. The next day, Princess Shireen who is underage is grabbed by soldiers, dragged to a wooden pyre, tied to a large stake in the middle, and burned alive in front of Stannis, Selyse, and Melissandre. The burning of Princess Shireen clearly is a form of torture, as it is purposely done to inflict pain with the consent of state officials as noted by Article 1 of the CAT.

Moreover, it is a violation of the Convention on the Rights of the Child. Article 2, Section 2 affirms that all states party to the convention ought to take appropriate measures to ensure the protection of children from "discrimination or punishment" (OHCHR 1990). This protection from punishment is explained further under Article 19, Section 1 of the convention that explains how all children ought to be protected from all forms of "physical or mental violence" and "maltreatment or exploitation . . . while in the care of parents(s)" (OHCHR 1990). In Princess Shireen's case, she was a child unprotected from punishment, physical and mental violence, and exposed to maltreatment by being burned alive while in the care of her parents. Hence, it is an extreme example of a case that represents an overlapping violation of the standards of human rights from the CAT and the Convention on the Rights of the Child.

Even in instances when the child has voluntarily chosen to face situations that may involve exposing them to human rights violations, the situation that confronts the child is still a violation of the Convention on the Rights of the Child. During the final season of *Game of Thrones*, the living are involved in a battle against the White Walkers and the Army of the Dead. The most prominent characters in the series join for the common cause to fight against the dead, including Lady Lyanna Mormont, who is thirteen years old. Her participation in war constitutes a violation of Article 38 of the Convention on the Rights of the Child that prevents any children from being directly involved in armed conflict or refrains any state parties to recruit children (OHCHR 1990). Moreover, the process of her death when she is squeezed to death in the hand of a club-wielding giant can constitute torture and a violation of Article 1 of the convention, as Lady Mormont suffers severe physical pain and is punished by the giant for being a part of the army of Daenerys Targaryen.

Along with the overlapping violations of various treaties, the series also provides examples of multiple overlapping violations, namely Article 1 and Article 10, from the CAT. This is particularly the case in the final episode of Season 6. Cersei Lannister is crowned the queen of the Seven Kingdoms after taking back control of the city from the religious group, the Sparrows, that had once imprisoned her. After Cersei returns to power, she imprisons the nun Septa Unella from the Sparrows who forced Cersei's confession, ordered her solitary confinement, tortured her with beating, starved her, and presided over her walk of atonement which Cersei was forced to do without clothes. Septa Unella's own behavior, which is briefly referenced, is an act of torture and ill-treatment, as it forced a confession out of Cersei and deprived her of her basic human rights. Cersei tortures Septa Unella in a similar way by strapping the nun immobile to a table and waterboarding her with wine. Waterboarding is a form of psychological and physical torture as noted by UN Special Rapporteur Nils Melzer (OHCHR 2017) and by the OHCHR (2011). The scene takes a turn for the worse with Ser Gregor, the knight who protects Cersei, being called in as the official "interrogator" of Septa Unella. Ser Gregor is known for his nonhuman-like qualities and brutal violent techniques of killing, and although the scene transitions and does not show what really happens to Septa Unella, it is understood from the screams coming out of the prison cell that she will likely be subject to crueler practices of torture. Ser Gregor's position as the new torturer is a violation of Article 10 of the convention, as there is no education provided to prevent torture for those who are engaged in interrogation.

The final season of the series culminates in a horrific episode of torture and ill-treatment, one that violates a multitude of articles from the CAT. Article 1 that defines torture and ill-treatment, Article 2's provisions on how even in a state of war or a threat of war torture cannot be justified, and Article 4's explanation that states must ensure that torture is made punishable. In the battle of King's Landing—the final war of Daenerys Targaryen against Cersei Lannister for the control of the continent of Westeros, Daenerys's army and dragon kill a significant portion of Cersei's mercenary army (i.e., the Golden Company) and the Iron Fleet, and make way into the city. Although the Lannister soldiers surrender and Daenerys is asked to keep her promise of letting the civilians inside the city gates remain unharmed, she refuses and burns the entire city. The casualties include women, children, the elderly, and soldiers who have surrendered. After the battle is won, Daenerys justifies her actions and accountability is put aside until Jon Snow self-delivers a form of "justice" with the killing of Daenerys. The series discusses the history of family grievances and personality differences between Cersei and Daenerys to set the scene for the burning of the city. However, the act that involves the killing of civilians and is purposefully taken to inflict pain on an innocent population are forms of torture and ill-treatment that are not justifiable via the CAT.

Various aspects of torture and ill-treatment are replete throughout the series. The rich insight into the types of torture and ill-treatment techniques in the series, both physical and psychological, helps visualize these instances and shows similarities to events that transpire in international relations.

CONVENTION ON THE ELIMINATION OF ALL FORMS OF DISCRIMINATION AGAINST WOMEN (CEDAW)

Along with the CAT, the CEDAW set the parameters for other forms of human rights, particularly those related to women's rights. Often referred to as the International Bill of Rights for Women, CEDAW was adopted in 1979 by the United Nations General Assembly. Some of the human rights norms included in the convention are the guarantee and enjoyment of "human rights and fundamental freedoms" equal to that of men (Article 3); modification of "social and cultural patterns of conduct of men and women" to eliminate "prejudices" and customs on the "idea of inferiority or the superiority of either of the sexes" (Article 5, Section A); the prohibition of "all forms of traffic in women and exploitation of prostitution of women" (Article 6); and the equality of women and men to "freely choose a spouse and to enter into marriage only with their free and full consent" (Article 16, Section 2) (UN Women 2018). Underlying these human rights guidelines are the emphasis on equality and nondiscrimination of women and men.

The convention defines discrimination against women as "any distinction, exclusion or restriction made on the basis of sex which has the effect or purpose of impairing or nullifying the recognition, enjoyment or exercise by women, irrespective of their marital status, on a basis of equality of men and women, of human rights and fundamental freedoms in the political, economic, social, cultural, civil or any other field" (UN Women 2018). States party to the CEDAW are expected to take appropriate measures that prohibit discrimination, which may include legislative changes.

Discrimination, although not explicitly stated in the convention, is interpreted as also covering violence against women. States party to the convention are expected to prohibit any practices that constitute such forms of violence (UN Women 2018). The Committee on the Elimination of All Forms of Discrimination Against Women, the monitoring body of CEDAW with mandates defined under the Article 17 through 30 of the convention, further explains the connections between discrimination and violence against women. The committee's General Recommendation Number 19 adopted in 1992 (HRI/GEN/1/Rev.8) categorizes "gender-based violence" as a "form of discrimination that seriously inhibits women's ability to enjoy rights and freedoms on a basis of equality with men" (UN Committee 1992). The discrimination is purposely directed against women to inflict "physical, mental or sexual harm or suffering" simply because she is a woman (UN Committee 1992).

The committee defines sexual harassment, traditional practices perpetuated by culture that are harmful to the health of women, and compulsory sterilization or abortion as examples of discrimination and sexual violence against women (UN Committee 1992). This definition has some overlapping resonance with the description of torture from the CAT on the purposeful infliction of pain. In fact, UN Special Rapporteurs on the CAT have long concluded that sexual violence can amount to torture and ill-treatment. According to the 2008 Report of the Special Rapporteur to the Human Rights Council of the General Assembly (A/HRC/7/3), "rape constitutes torture when it is carried out by, at the instigation of, or with the consent or acquiescence of public officials (OHCHR 2008). Such views are also reiterated in the Committee on CEDAW's General Recommendation. The committee elaborates on CEDAW's Article 16 on the rights established in marriage as it relates to rape. According to the committee, "family violence is one of the most insidious forms of violence against women" and includes "battering, rape, other forms of sexual assault, mental and other forms of violence" (UN Committee 1992). It is understood that states party to CEDAW will adopt measures to prevent such forms of sexual violence against women.

The conducts of discrimination and violence against women as outlined by CEDAW and the committee that monitors the CEDAW's implementation, provides a unique set of principles on women's rights to analyze the developments in *Game of Thrones*. On multiple occasions characters are seen violating Article 6 which prohibits prostitution, Article 16 on marriage-related rights, and other guidelines from the Committee on CEDAW related to family violence, rape, and sexual harassment. The first instance appears on Season 1, Episode 2, when Prince Viserys Targaryen arranges the marriage of his sister Princess Daenerys Targaryen against her will to Khal Drogo of the Dotharki tribe. For the exchange, Viserys is set to receive an army of 40,000 men from Drogo who will then be used for Viserys's invasion of Westeros. The wedding arrangement is a violation of Article 16, Section 2 of CEDAW, as Daenerys is denied the right to "freely choose a spouse" and is forced into marriage against her "free and full consent" (UN Women 2018).

Additionally, the first sexual intercourse that Daenerys has on her wedding night is another violation of women's rights. The wedding night's scene involves a terrified Daenerys who is raped against her will by her husband Khal Drogo. While rape is not explicitly stated, Daenerys's pain-stricken face the next morning leaves the audience to reasonably conclude a forced intercourse situation. This is a form of sexual violence against women, which the Committee on CEDAW discussed as necessitating the intervention of state parties to "establish support services for victims of family violence" (UN Committee 1992). In Daenerys's case, her rape becomes a habitual practice from Drogo and she, as the victim, is not provided with any support to be protected from such circumstances.

The rape of Daenerys from Khal Drogo is one of many instances of sexual violence throughout Season 1 that feature the Dotharki tribe. Others include, for instance, sexual harassment and battery that threatens the safety of women and rape of women from villages that the Dotharki pillage and conquer. These scenes in Season 1, Episode 8 are depicted as part of the tribe's culture of war. The mass rape and sexual harassment carried out by the Dotharki, who now exercise political control over the conquered villages, constitute violations of the General Recommendation 19 of the Committee on CEDEAW and constitute a form of torture as noted by the CAT.

Additional cases of rape and family violence are also present in Season 5, Episode 6 during Ramsay Bolton and Sansa Stark's wedding. On the night of the wedding, Ramsay rapes Sansa. The layer of sexual violence is intensified as Ramsay forces Theon Greyjoy (who is serving Ramsay) to watch the rape. The situation is a violation of women's rights not only due to the rape, but also represents the most "insidious forms of violence against women" (UN Committee 1992) as it also involves mental violence against Sansa. She is forced to endure the sexual violence and understand that the scene is being watched by another man, Greyjoy. Although Sansa is not a prostitute, the setting of this scene places her in a form of exploitation and prostitution against her will, which is a violation of Article 6 of the CAT (UN Women 2018).

The list of women's rights' violations in the series continues throughout Season 2. In Season 2, Episode 4, King Joffrey is offered a "gift" of two prostitutes, Ros and Daisy, from his uncle Tyrion Lannister. While Joffrey is startled at the very beginning, he soon decides to relish his pleasures not related to sexual intercourse. He asks one of the women to hit the other using a leather belt, then proceeds with handing her a piece of wood to continue the beating, and eventually brings a crossbow into the bedchamber to force Ros to beat Daisy unconscious. Daisy's body is later dumped in Tyrion Lannister's chamber and in the latter episodes of the season, Ros is found dead with multiple crossbow wounds struck against her body. The "exploitation of prostitution of women" present in the episode is a violation of Article 6 of CEDAW (UN Women 2018). And, as the women are subject to a different status and deprived of their rights due to their status of being women, such acts are a form of discrimination against women and a violation of Article 3 of CEDAW (UN Women 2018).

Moreover, the "physical, mental, or sexual" violence that Ros and Daisy suffer is an example of a form of sexual violence and discrimination as noted by the Committee on CEDAW (UN Committee 1992). As these acts inflict physical trauma and mental pain and suffering, they also constitute a violation of the CAT. Similar violations are present in Episode 10 of the same season, during a scene when Brienne of Tarth leads the captive Jaime Lannister through the Riverlands. The two come across the corpses of three women hanging from a tree, with a sign around their necks that states "they lay with lions." The women were beaten and killed by soldiers loyal to the Stark family for the "sin" of having engaged in sexual intercourse with the soldiers from the Lannister family. Such degrading treatment of women, which disregards their rights for being women and inflicts physical and mental pain, are violations of Article 3 of CEDAW and Article 1 of the CAT.

The instances of women's rights violations in the televised series present a category of discrimination and sexual violence that overlap human rights standards defined in the CEDAW, CAT, and the Recommendations from the Committee on CEDAW. The layers of discrimination and violence against women represents the exacerbation of the treatment of women in the feudal societal context of *Game of Thrones*. The cases also adequately portray the patriarchal and discriminatory power relationships and socialized gender stereotypes which although set in a feudal context may have some resonance to contemporary international political contexts.

CONCLUSION

Through the examination of two specific human rights instruments that deal with torture and women's rights, this chapter presented how international legal instruments of human rights can be applied to analyze *Game of Thrones*. While none of the international legal frameworks on human rights are established in the period and setting of *Game of Thrones*, the characters that are violating human rights are portrayed as amoral, unethical, and at times even irrational. Such characterization indicates that despite the absence of human rights norms in the feudal context of the televised series, there may be some parallels on the standards of morality in the fiction and international politics today. In other words, there does seem to be an understanding of what constitute "principled norms," which are norms based on "beliefs of right and wrong, such as norms of human rights" (Clark 2001, 11).

Even without the "moral beliefs rooted in the Western liberal conception of human dignity" which is articulated in the Universal Declaration of Human Rights (Clark 2001, 11), there is a preexisting expectation in *Game of Thrones* of what is correct or wrong in terms of human behavior. This includes how torture, ill-treatment, sexual violence, and discrimination against women are depicted as abusive behaviors against human rights, even without the existence of the CAT and the CEDAW in *Game of Thrones*. The characterization of the perpetrators of human rights violations as vile, distorted, cunning, and power-hungry individuals creates an imagery of the human rights violator as the problematic subject, one who is challenging the victim who is benign and relatively in a powerless position.

While the analysis of this chapter did not touch upon this aspect further, these evil characters always face some level of violence themselves as the series proceeds. These developments are a form of accountability that is rendered upon the perpetrators by the series' producers, who by weighing in on the debate of morality side with the need to respect the fundamental human rights of all individuals. This is precisely the reason why the series becomes a useful tool to understand various types of human rights violations, as they help visualize the instances and even with the assumption of a fictional reality, they establish how each scene challenges an individuals' dignity and human rights.

NOTES

1. This is not to neglect the importance of the emergence of formal legal expressions of human rights in the pre–World War II period, specifically worker's rights (or labor rights) that accompanied the International Labor Organization's creation in 1919 (i.e., Forced Labor Convention of 1930 and the Freedom of Association and Protection of the Right to Organize Convention of 1948, among other things) (Macklem 2015). However, it is undeniable that World War II was the pivotal critical juncture from which human rights legal standards proliferated at a greater rate than had been previously present in the international system.

2. Throughout the chapter the Universal Declaration of Human Rights will be referred to as either the UDHR, the Declaration, or in its full official name.

3. *Opinio juris* here refers to an opinion of law or a statement of legal obligation, which is necessary to establish a legally binding custom (as a part of customary international law). For more information on *opinion juris*, please see Shelton (2000).

SIX

Indigenous Peoples

Among the more prominent thematic studies of international relations that focus on the international political economy, security, conflict resolution, peace, foreign policy, and human rights, the study of underrepresented populations and their politics of identity is one that is regarded as a niche field; one that blurs the lines between domestic and international events. This is especially true for the study of Indigenous populations. The inclusion and importance of Indigenous peoples in conversations of international relations has mainly been present in works that address human rights or in literature on individual state matters related to sovereignty. Even within these subcategories, they are a marginalized population, a separated study if you will, from the dominant discourse on human rights norms, theories of human rights, and conceptualizations of statehood and sovereignty. In part, this reflects the field of international relations that has unfortunately "internalized many of the enabling narratives of colonialism" and has failed to "take notice of Indigenous peoples" (Beier 2005, 2).

Colonialism in the discipline has its roots in the settler-state mentality that regards Indigenous peoples as not constituting "authentic political communities" (Beier 2005, 15). The settler mentality refers to the dominant position of a group of population that creates a hierarchical relationship of power between the colonizing settler power and the colonial subjects, who are the Indigenous population. Hence, the absence of research in international relations that includes Indigenous peoples as political actors and neglects their presence in any political discourse is one that reproduces this settler-state idea of colonialism. It is a discipline that voices the perspective of the dominant society, one which examines the world from a Western Eurocentric perspective. It is also one that describes Indigenous people as the "primitive peoples of the world" who

89

have "no texts to be analyzed" and who are an uncivilized society do not necessitate or deserve a separate empirical examination for research (Beier 2005, 67).

As Indigenous populations continue their demand towards recognition in the international political sphere, making their cause far from insignificant, it is important to focus on this group of peoples, the politics that has shaped their identity and their presence in international politics. This chapter focuses on the Indigenous peoples' position in international politics to address this void in the field. The chapter does not dive deep into the conceptual debates on who constitutes Indigenous peoples, which often involves studies of Indigenous peoples as those who no longer have control over their land, politics, or independence (Alfred and Wilmer 1997) and who are the "conquered descendants of earlier inhabitants of a region . . . whose traditional social, economic, and cultural customs . . . are sharply distinct from those of dominant groups" (Gurr 2000, 17). Rather, it attempts to broadly understand the approach of the international community toward the question and concept of indigeneity. This is based from the perspective on how Indigenous populations are defined in the academy by "negation" as primitive peoples of the world who are sidelined in terms of their culture, society, and politics (Beier 2005, 67). More specifically, it discusses the role of settler-colonial mentality in shaping the construction of characteristics of the Indigenous population, which includes some discussions of intersections of hierarchy of political power, race as a social construction, and socioeconomic class.

The chapter refers to a group of population present in *Game of Thrones*, the Dothraki. The Dothraki do not conform to the exact experience of colonialization in the modern political realm. Nor do they fit the specific concerns made in reference to Indigenous peoples, on the dispossession of "lands, territories, and resources" and the historical injustices they have suffered (UN 2007). Nonetheless, the way they are portrayed (for instance their physique, livelihood, and culture), the role they take, and their interactions with other actors in the series personify, in part, some of the characteristics of Indigenous population and the challenges they face in contemporary politics. Their interactions with others also reflect a type of the relationship between the settler-colonial and the marginalized other, who are portrayed as primitive, uncivilized, underdeveloped, and therefore not deserving of the same level of respect in treatment. The references to such descriptions toward the Dothraki are present in the series, and therefore make the population comparable to that of the Indigenous peoples in contemporary politics.

INDIGENOUS PEOPLES IN INTERNATIONAL POLITICS

International relations scholarship perceives the Indigenous peoples' demand for inclusion in the international political discourse as a challenge to the status quo of international order. This is in part since the implementation of "indigenous rights requires a rethinking and reordering" of dominant concepts of statehood, regarding "sovereignty, territoriality, decolonization" (Lightfoot 2016, 4). By sovereignty, we refer to a definition that is socially constructed and which includes elements of the legal recognition by other states, juridical independence, autonomy from external interference, and the ability of a state to exert control over the activities both within and across its borders (Krasner 2009, 15). The Indigenous peoples' identity, their non-state actor status, and their social movement that transcends state boundaries may represent a perceived threat to sovereignty for states (Niezen 2003).

From American Indian studies to global Indigenous studies, the category of what constitutes indigeneity is also seen in similar ways. Indigeneity marks an "intellectual project" that questions the "Euro-American constructions of self" and the "nation-state" that underwrites liberal democracies (Byrd and Rothberg 2011, 3). It reframes boundaries and notions of traditional political space. In fact, some scholars suggest that the Indigenous actors fight for a third space (Bruyneel 2007). This space is the recognition of the existence of a sovereign area within the context of another sovereign state. These ideas are considered as a form of resistance from settler-states, such as that of the United States, that have previously imposed temporal and spatial limitations on Indigenous groups (Bruyneel 2007).

Indigenous studies, particularly concerning the struggle with how to articulate the "tensions between overweening colonial power and resilient, resistant actors," can at times be also connected with the conceptualization of the "subaltern" (Byrd and Rothberg 2011, 6). The subaltern here refers to the elusive figures in capitalist society, or the oppressed subject (e.g., the women workers who are participants of production but whose presence is only acknowledged in death or whose course of development is determined for her by other outside political entities).

Even when marginalized populations, such as Indigenous people and subaltern gender groups in society attempt to speak or voice their positions (i.e., Spivak's reading of the suicide of the young woman Bhubaneswari Bhaduri in Calcutta, India, during the 1920s [Spivak 1999, 247]), their voices are not heard (Byrd and Rothberg 2011, 5). The gap between the sender and receiver of the message reflects the hierarchical power difference between the groups on both ends. The "failed reception" has to do with the nonrecognition of the marginalized or subaltern other from the dominant group (Byrd and Rothberg 2011, 6). Such ideas are reflected in Indigenous-settler colonial relationships. For instance, in settler-colonial states such as the United States, there is an effort to impose "economic, legal, and political institutions" on Indigenous peoples, including the "jurisdictional authority over territory" (Bruyneel 2007, 217). The Indigenous population are the subaltern group that resist this imposition of the settler-state, speaking against the boundaries of colonial rule.

In the practice of international politics, the manifestation of this settler-colonial and Indigenous populations' relationship becomes clearer, even in the process of establishing international legal norms that protects Indigenous peoples. One of the manifestations of the position of Indigenous peoples in international politics occurred during the passage of the United Nations Declaration on the Rights of Indigenous Peoples (UNDRIP) in 2007. While 143 states from the total of 193 states of the General Assembly of the United Nations voted in favor of the UNDRIP, four states voted against the declaration. These four—Australia, Canada, New Zealand, and the United States were settler-states with Indigenous populations. The reasoning for their opposition was due to the provisions of "land rights and self-determination, including the principle of free, prior, and informed consent" (Lightfoot 2016, 2). By self-determination, these states were referring to the right of Indigenous people to "freely determine their political status and freely pursue their economic, social, and cultural development" as noted under Article 3 of the UNDRIP and previously referenced in Article 1 of the International Covenant on Civil and Political Rights passed in 1966 (UN 2007; OHCHR 1966). The four states' reference to land and prior consent dealt with the protection of Indigenous peoples' lands and livelihoods, whereby states must have "consent" from Indigenous peoples prior to undertaking development projects and activities in Indigenous lands (OHCHR 2013).

These two principles recognized Indigenous people as legitimate political actors. The disapproval of the UNDRIP by the four states on grounds of self-determination, land rights, and prior-consultation, sheds light on the difficulties Indigenous peoples have in political recognition in settler-states, as a group deserving of protection in international politics. Particularly, Canada's position in opposing the declaration raised questions as to whether the state was simply trying to "keep control of the vast resources on land claimed by aboriginal communities" (CBC 2007, Article 7, Section 3).

Despite the initial four-state opposition, the UNDRIP passed. In fact, Canada officially changed its position and adopted the UNDRIP in 2016. In 2010, the United States endorsed the UNDRIP. The UNDRIP's provisions were further supported by an internationally legally binding document from the International Labor Organization (ILO) Convention 169 that highlights the "importance of indigenous peoples' participation in decision-making, land issues and environmental, social and economic developments" (Lindroth and Sinevaara-Niskanen 2018, 5–6). The ILO Convention 169 also guarantees the rights and freedoms of Indigenous peoples without "hindrance or discrimination" (ILO 2017). Regional international documents, such as the American Declaration on the Rights of Indigenous Peoples further reinforced the rights of Indigenous peoples, urging states to adopt measures to "eradicate all forms of violence and discrimination, particularly against indigenous women" (Indian Law 2017).

If one were to analyze the record of compliance with these international instruments that promised change and protection of Indigenous peoples, there continues to be numerous shortcomings of the inclusion of Indigenous peoples' interests in international politics. The UNDRIP and the American Declaration are nonlegally binding and only twenty-two states have ratified the ILO Convention 169. States continue to violate Indigenous peoples' rights, including settler-states such as Canada that have not yet addressed the basic rights of Indigenous peoples to have access to clean drinking water (Coletta 2018). The violations are also present in states with significant Indigenous populations, such as Peru, (where impunity continues for the 2009 Bagua Massacre when police clashed with Indigenous Amazonian people protesting the US–Peru Free Trade Agreement provisions on occupation of Indigenous peoples' land and exploitation of natural resources in Bagua) (Amnesty International 2017). Hence, while Indigenous peoples may have been provided a "seat at the tables of global politics" with these international legal developments (Lindroth and Sinevaara-Niskanen 2018, 6), the lack of enforcement of Indigenous peoples' rights at the domestic level reflects the unchanged dynamics of the subaltern marginalized Indigenous population with the dominant settler-state in contemporary international politics.

THE INDIGENOUS

The ethnographic works of European missionaries and colonial administrators that documented their encounters with the Indigenous population had a prolonged impact in shaping the discourse on the Indigenous population and the European settler-state. The writings took on a European settler-state perspective, speaking from an "authoritative voice" about the contact with the "native" population, who were seen as lacking "attributes of advanced societies" (Beier 2005, 67). The established hierarchy was of European superiority vis-à-vis that of the inferior Indigenous population. Such ideas continued with Christopher Columbus's journal of his first voyage (1492–1493) written over five hundred years ago. The text remains relevant for shaping the narrative toward the Indigenous peoples in international politics. Specifically, it provides a glimpse of the relationship between the settler-colonial state and the Indigenous population, as one that is characterized by fixated adjectives on the physique. On multiple occasions, Columbus writes about the naked appearance of the Indigenous population. The "natives" were "as naked as when their mothers bore them" and the women went "without any covering" (Columbus 1893, 106, 113). Not all Indigenous populations bore little clothing as had been described by Columbus, as for instance the Incan Empire emphasized distinct clothing, adornments, and hairstyles to differentiate the nobility from the common folk. Such details were noted by other settler-colonials such as Miguel de Estete who was among the first Europeans to see Cuzco, Peru, and even the conquistador Pedro Pizarro. Nonetheless, the associations of the Indigenous population and the absence of clothing propagated rapidly with Columbus's journal. And, European settler-colonials further established the connection of how nakedness of the Indigenous population was a sign of wildness and inferiority, while the European civilization with proper garments represented the superior culture (Graubart 2007, 40). For this reason, the process of wearing clothes, particularly European or Western attire, became an "important component of the civilizing process" of the Indigenous population by the settler-colonials (Graubart 2007, 40–41).

In *Game of Thrones*, there is one group that is portrayed in a similar light of inferiority to that of the other kingdoms. Often, the ideas of their civility and primitivity are related to their appearance, including the garments they wear. This group is the Dothraki. The Dothraki reside in the continent of Essos, which is separate from the continent of Westeros. The Dothraki are characterized as a nomadic group of population. From the moment they are introduced in Season 1 Episode 1, the Dothraki appear shirtless, riding on horses, sporting a long beard and hair, with dark features. These traits are portrayed in contrast with the Targaryen family from the continent of Westeros, whose presence among the Dothraki is manifested with Daenerys Targaryen (who has been forced into marriage with Khal Drogo of the Dothraki by her brother Viserys Targaryen). Daenerys is portrayed as a woman of fair complexion, blonde hair, clothed, and one that is not used to riding on horses, traveling long distances, and living in nomadic tents.

The differentiation of the continental origin of the Dothraki and the Targaryen family, and subsequently their stark contrast of skin complexion, physique, attire, and living conditions, alludes to a difference in ethnic portrayals that were present from the period of Columbus' voyages. Particularly, it resonates with the ideas of how nakedness and the less amount of clothing are associated with a population who are uncivilized, wild, and non-Western (Graubart 2007; Columbus 1893). Such ideas are affirmed in Episode 2 of Season 1 during Daenerys and Khal Drogo's wedding night. The intimate encounter of sexual intercourse between Daenerys and Khal Drogo is portrayed in an animalesque manner. There is little conversation exchanged between Khal Drogo and Daenerys, Khal Drogo then forces himself upon Daenerys whose clothes are brusquely torn, and the scene then changes to show Daenerys waking up in the morning with a pain-stricken face implying domestic abuse and rape.

The tearing of the clothes, which symbolizes Daenerys's class, stature, and association with the Targaryen family and the continent of Westeros represents the defiance the Dothraki pose upon the "civilized" population. Additionally, the absence of conversation and the physical imposition of the Dothraki leader Khal Drogo on Daenerys reflects an inverted dynamic of power of the uncivilized Dothraki upon the "civilized" Targaryen family. Simultaneously, the inference of rape from the wedding night confirm the "wildness" of the Dothraki which again includes parallels to the Indigenous populations' portrayal in the eyes of the European colonial settlers.

The portrayal of violence is another perpetuated myth that adds to the characterization of the Indigenous population as savage-like beings who challenge the settler-colonials. In the context of the Wild West and the Western accounts in the United States, there is an opposed construction and distorted social reality about the violent behavior of the Indigenous population. Despite the documented evidence in history, the Indigenous are depicted as violent, aggressive populations (Dorris 1987). The danger includes the widely professed rape narrative of the Indigenous men against the white Euro-American women. However, according to historical documents there were very few instances of rape by the Indigenous population. Many "Native American nations had strict proscriptions against mixing sex and war" (Block 2006, 225). Indigenous male encounters with Euro-American women would take place only during contexts of war or conflict. Thus the likelihood of rape occurring simultaneously would highly be unlikely. Nonetheless, the stories continued depicting Anglo-American women as vulnerable and under possible attack by "nonwhite New World residents," such as the Indigenous people who were considered "savage" and "threatened to overwhelm" the colonies (Block 2006, 218).

The rendering of the Indigenous as a "dangerous" population is "integral to the (re)production of the settler state" as it legitimizes their violent reaction against the Indigenous people and it also establishes a "superiority of the forces that overcame it" (Beier 2005, 138). Moreover, the association of the Indigenous with danger, savage-behavior, and unprecedented violence sets them apart from the contrasting population of the settler-colonials who are civilized and not untamed.

Violence is what accompanies the depiction of the Dothraki population in *Game of Thrones*. From the beginning of Season 1, these ideas are set in place during an exchange between King Robert Baratheon and his then-wife Queen Cersei Lannister. When pondering the danger that Daenerys Targaryen and her husband Khal Drogo's Dothraki might pose to King's Landing, King Robert discusses the stereotypes that are associated with the Dothraki warriors. According to him, the Dothraki loot livestock and crops, burn towns, "kill every man who can't hide behind a stone wall" and even enslave women and children. Such ideas of brutality are an association that is primarily done with the Dothraki, although the series later reveals of the brutalities committed by other individuals from the Seven Kingdoms, for instance the Lannisters (i.e., Jaime Lannister throws Bran Stark out the window of a castle and renders him crippled). These ideas continue to play out during the series, marginalizing the Dothraki as the group more linked with danger and threat.

During Season 1, Episode 8, the Dothraki pillage the Lhazareen Village. The village men (who are referred to as the "lamb men") are taken as slaves, to be sold to slave traders in return for gold, silk, and steel for the Dothraki. Although the Dothraki do not believe in gold or riches, they trade the "lamb men" for gold to hire ships and sail to Westeros for Daenerys to claim her throne. Hence, the motivation for the Dothraki violence is rooted not necessarily in their own violent predispositions. In this case it is due to Daenerys's own political ambition of power. Nonetheless, such ideas are absent from the episode. In fact, the scenes focus more on the physical use of force from the Dothraki warriors against the women from the Lhazareen Village that seek to claim them as their prize for war. When Daenerys stops this behavior, she is challenged by Dothraki warriors. She asks Khal Drogo of the reason for the women enslavement and rape, Khal Drogo replies, "This is the way of war" and that the women from captured villages are (sex) "slaves" as had been the tradition of Dothraki war. It is only after Daenerys asks Khal Drogo to forgo such acts, that he considers making an exception for the Lhazareen Village women (*Game of Thrones*, Season 1, Episode 8). Infliction of violence on women is not limited to the Dothraki. However, it is emphasized as an innate quality of the Dothraki ways of war which is different than the instances of rape present in the series throughout the other Seven Kingdoms (e.g., Queen Cersei Lannister's rape from her husband in Season 1).

The emphasis on how rape and female enslavement are part of the war culture of the Dothraki is similar to the characterization of Indigenous peoples in the United States' context, as violent men who are going to threaten Anglo-American women (Block 2006). What is more unique about this particular example of the Dothraki and the possible rape of Lhazareen Village women is the intervention of Daenerys Targaryen, whose identity is more associated with the settler-colonial or the civilized population in the series. After she "reasons" with her husband, the Dothraki leader considers halting the violence. Although these developments are not a takeover of the Dothraki, which would be more commonplace by a settler-colonial state that legitimates their violence against the Indigenous population and establishes a "superiority of the forces that overcame it" (Beier 2005, 138), it nonetheless can be interpreted as the establishment of Daenerys Targaryen's superiority above that of the Dothraki, whose culture of war included rape and enslavement, more closely aligned with uncivilized behavior.

The second instance of violence with the Dothraki is another which involves the role of Daenerys Targaryen. In Season 1, Episode 6 during a feast the Dothraki are having, Viserys Targaryen threatens his sister Daenerys Targaryen, Khal Drogo, and their unborn child. Viserys wants to take part in the "whore's feast" which he is denied by Khal Drogo who directs him toward the back of the tent. The instance provokes Viserys who points a sword at Daenery's pregnant belly. The instigator of the violence in the scene was Viserys Targaryen. However, the series spends more time on detailing the punishment that Viserys receives from Khal Drogo, which in part was instructed by Daenerys Targaryen. Khal Drogo melts his belt of gold medallions in a pot and Viserys is showered with the hot liquid gold from his head which leads to his instant death. Daenerys had given Khal Drogo the idea of the golden crown, and yet Khal Drogo is seen as the executor of the harsh punishment. This adds to the depiction of the Dothraki as the vicious, aggressive, and savage population that are able to tolerate such forms of violence.

A deeper analysis of Dothraki culture reveals that Khal Drogo agreed to Daenerys's idea to hold the festivities at Vaes Dothrak, a sacred place for the Dothraki where spilling blood is considered sacrilegious. Hence, the killing with melted gold would fulfill the work of punishment without spilling any blood. Nonetheless, such references are not explicitly mentioned; hence, only the melting gold punishment behavior again is put in contrast with the rest of the developments in the same episode, where this level of violence is only correspondent to the Dothraki scenes.

Language also becomes a key aspect of colonial related discourse that characterizes the Indigenous population with noncivility or underdevelopment and the European or Western colonial settlers with modernity. Rules of who are included as part of the civilized group or belonging to the "colonizer's culture" is based on "language, art, political structures, [and] social conventions," which includes the type of political institutions, clothing as social conventions, and language of the colonial power (Ashcroft, Griffiths, and Tiffin 2000, 35). The absence of these characteristics is related to the colonized population. Particularly the Indigenous populations are often characterized as having distinct "social structures and cultural histories," which are "primitive" and "uncivilized." This contrasts modern states which prefer to be associated with "development" and "modernization" (Ashcroft, Griffiths, and Tiffin 2000, 35; Wilmer 1993, 36–37). Therefore, the manifestation of this group in politics is not regarded as a positive factor from the state's perspective, as their absence would be regarded as bringing the state closer to a more developed economic, cultural, and social status in world politics.

In *Game of Thrones*, the majority of the population speak the Common Tongue, which is spoken in English for the television audience. This includes the Seven Kingdoms of the continent of Westeros: the North (House Stark), the Vale (House Arryn), the Riverlands (House Tully), the Stormlands (House Baratheon), the Westerlands (House Lannister), the Reach (House Tyrell), the Principality of Dorne (House Martell), and even the Iron Islands (Greyjoys of Pyke) which is a separate independent kingdom. The other separate language group is Valyrian, which includes High Valyrian and Low Valyrian. High Valyrian is a "dead language used as the language of learning and education among the nobility of Essos and Westeros" (Laskowski 2017, para. 10). This equates in modern days to Latin and its position in terms of being associated with high culture from the older generations. The Valyrian languages are spoken by the Targaryens (e.g., Daenerys), and among the Red Priests in Season 3, Episode 6 of *Game of Thrones*, when they need to discuss matters related to the Lord of Light, the god they serve. Aside from these languages, the Dothraki have a unique position in being one of the only population with a language of their own. Different from Valyrian that is related to a cultured class and those who share similar physical complexions with others from the Seven Kingdoms, Dothraki's language is exclusive to the population and one that is associated with a foreign group distinct from others.

The Indigenous populations in contemporary politics are characterized as having a separate language and culture which is different than the majority population, and is categorized as uncivilized and primitive (Ashcroft, Griffiths, and Tiffin 2000; Wilmer 1993). Given the physical characterization of the Dothraki that already differentiates them from others, the linguistic barrier that is introduced between the Common Tongue and the Dothraki strikes a stronger contrast than those who speak Varlyian. There are also parallels to draw out about the Indigenous populations and their languages in modern politics and the similar ways that the Dothraki language is portrayed in the series. The language is not a language of the nobility nor of the fair complexioned Targaryens. Rather, it is a language of the nomadic people, those who are not clothed, and ride horses. Therefore, the language of the Dothraki reifies the relationship of hierarchy between the settler-colonial and the Indigenous population, one where the dominant language of English and the Common Tongue are regarded as superior and the Dothraki's own language are relegated to an inferior status.

CONCLUSION

The characterization of Indigenous populations as the "other," the group that is in violent conflict with the settler-colonials, is a long-lasting depiction that has shaped the discourse on the Indigenous population within global politics. As a population that is not part of the group in power, one which has a separate notion of space, territory, customs, and traditions from the dominant majority, this group is seen as a negated population. It is a group of people whose identities are exploited for political gains from the dominant group, the roots of which can be traced back to the imperialist conquest and early postconquest colonial days of settlement. More often than not they are associated with primitivity, savagery, uncivilized behavior, and animalesque-like qualities of physique, in contrast with the European individual. The colonizer takes on the role of the civilized, rational, and reason-based culture, which is seen as being the superior one that has been able to conquer the territories of the Indigenous population despite not needing to inflict as much grotesque-like forms of violence as the Indigenous people. At the underlying surface of these ideas are notions of settler-colonial superiority and Indigenous inferiority that are established.

In similar ways, the Dothraki population in *Game of Thrones* depicts these stigmatized visions of the Indigenous peoples in contemporary international relations. They are portrayed as having a vicious war culture, although other kingdoms in the series also engage in similar violent behavior. The Dothraki are depicted as people who loot, pillage, kill, and rape women. Even when they stop their behavior short of committing such brutalities, they continue to be associated with such heinous acts, while other prominent characters in the series (e.g., Lannisters) who too are responsible for the same type of crimes are portrayed as more civilized. Finally, the absence of clothing and a unique language sets the Dothraki apart from the Seven Kingdoms and the Iron Islands that speak the Common Tongue (English) and wear more clothing. As clothing and language are other identifiers of how those in power defined their interactions of superiority and inferiority with the Indigenous population in their first encounters from the 1400s, one can argue that in similar ways the Dothraki represent the Indigenous peoples in *Game of Thrones* and thus are treated in parallelly unfair ways.

Conclusion

The final season of *Game of Thrones* saw the White Walkers and their Army of the Dead face off with Jon Snow, King of the North, and the Kingdom of Daenerys Targaryen, Queen of the Andals, Meereen and Khaleesi of the Great Grass Sea, and the allies they have picked up along the way. Of course, one question everyone was asking at the start of the seasons was: Who will win what is being dubbed as "The Great War?" Before the season aired, we made predictions about the answer. Since it is clear war with the White Walkers is inevitable, we started with learning the power capabilities of each side.

It is not clear just how many men are in the Army of the Dead. But, as previously stated, it is a whole lot. Recall, the White Walkers and the Army of the Dead are not the same thing. The White Walkers are mystical beings and have humanoid characteristics. The Army of the Dead, on the other hand, are those corpses the White Walkers reanimate, also known as Wights. While the White Walkers exhibit superior intelligence, Wights appear to respond to commands from the White Walkers but lack any other signs of intellect.

The White Walkers have demonstrated their strength as a formidable power. They already successfully killed and turned one of Daenerys' dragons into an undead member of their army. The Army of the Dead also has giants which, of course, have a significant amount of strength not matched by one regular man. Wights also have superhuman strength. In addition, the Army of the Dead has the unique ability to continue to grow quickly, provided there are dead bodies around. The living take a lot longer to generate new people capable of fighting in a war. This gives the undead a strategic advantage because of their reanimation capabilities. On the flip side, though, if a White Walker is killed, any Wight that White Walker made is also killed. Thus, killing the right individual can result in greater casualties for the Army of the Dead whereas if you kill any one of the humans, no one else dies as a direct result. This is a huge weakness that can be exploited to the alliance's advantage if they are able to take out the King of the White Walkers.

Daenerys' kingdom has approximately 8,000 Unsullied and 150,000 Dothraki fighters. The North is significantly smaller with around 15,000–20,000 fighters, including the Wildlings. Others have joined the fight too, helping the alliance to increase its numbers. The Vale provides an additional 20,000 troops and the Reach contributes approximately

80,000. When you add the Greyjoys and others who have also aligned with the Kingdom of Daenerys and the North, the total number of fighting men is around 250,000 with approximately 100 ships in their fleet (Roberson 2016).

Daenerys also brings to the alliance two dragons; however, the White Walkers have proven that dragons pose little threat to them. They can snuff out their fire and, of course, Daenerys' third dragon was killed during an earlier battle with the White Walkers. The White Walkers reanimated it and now have it in their arsenal to use against the alliance (*Game of Thrones*, Season 7, Episode 6). While they are resistant to fire, it is not known if the White Walkers can withstand wildfire. As of right now, though, only King's Landing has that capability. Since they are not part of the alliance, it cannot be considered as part of the power capabilities of the alliance. The Wights, who make up the Army of the Dead, on the other hand, *are* resistant to fire. If the dragons can avoid the White Walkers, then they can pose a considerable threat to the number of undead in the White Walker's army.

White Walkers can be killed when stabbed by Valyrian steel or Dragonglass. Though both items are in short supply, Jon's efforts to mine as much as he could from Dragonstone have helped considerably to better arm the alliance (*Game of Thrones*, Season 7, Episode 4). Because stabbing the White Walkers and the Wights is a proven way to kill them, and because dragons can only inflict so much damage on their own, this means there is going to be some intense hand-to-hand combat that takes place in order to kill the White Walkers and defeat their army. High casualties are expected for both sides due to the closeness in match in terms of power capabilities. The use of wildfire could help tip the balance in favor of the alliance (though without Cersei's help wildfire is not an option), as, too, would someone with magical powers to compete with the magic of the White Walkers (though, again, no one has that capability). Without these things, as a result, the war will likely be decided by which side can hold out the longest while inflicting the greatest casualties, and, of course, who is the most skillful with a sword.

Given the above circumstances, this poses another important question: Will Cersei, Queen of King's Landing, join forces with the alliance, or will she remain neutral and wait for the war to weaken her adversaries so much that she is able to strike when they are at their most vulnerable, thereby consolidating her power over the Iron Throne? It seems the latter is most likely. There is an exception, though. If the White Walkers begin to pose a threat to King's Landing, Cersei will create at least a temporary alliance with the North and Daenerys' kingdom. This is because a rational actor will realize the defeat of the North and Daenerys' kingdom leaves King's Landing to fight the White Walkers' Army of the Dead on their own. Though its military is strong, it is unlikely King's Landing would be able to defeat the White Walkers, especially if the Army of the Dead was already successful at defeating the military prowess of the North and Daenerys' army and two dragons, and given the fact the White Walkers grow as they amass more dead bodies.

The prediction of an alliance between the three states, of course, rests on the assumption that Cersei is a rational actor. Some might question this based on previous actions. A realist, however, would argue her actions so far are calculated and rational. She is Queen of the Iron Throne after all. Is this not for what she has been vying all along? In short, if her power is threatened, Cersei will form an alliance. This willingness to do what it takes to survive, we believe, means she would even align herself with the White Walkers if, for some reason, they were to approach her and ask for an alliance. She would not hesitate to join with them to annihilate the North and Daenerys' kingdom since she knows if they defeat the White Walkers, they will turn on her next. The White Walkers, though, are in a position—both in terms of military prowess and strategic geographic location far enough away from King's Landing—such that they would not benefit from forming an alliance with Cersei.

Assuming the alliance of Jon, Daenerys, and company is successful at defeating the White Walkers and the Army of the Dead, with or without Cersei's help, what happens next? To answer in a truly political science fashion: It depends. How weakened are the North and the Kingdom of Daenerys? If it is severely weakened, then King's Landing can step in and overtake them militarily once again asserting its dominance over the Seven Kingdoms and consolidating Cersei's power as Queen of the Iron Throne. Even if an alliance with Cersei and the rest is formed to defeat the White Walkers, King's Landing will enter the fight late, if at all. If this is the case, casualties inflicted on King's Landing would potentially be much less than the other members of the alliance who have been embroiled in the battle for longer. This leaves King's Landing with the opportunity to exploit these weaknesses.

If, on the other hand, King's Landing is severely weakened compared to the other members of the alliance then, depending upon the balance of power, war between members of the alliance and King's Landing is likely. If the power balance is severely tilted in the favor of the alliance and not King's Landing, then war is less likely as King's Landing will likely attempt to reach some sort of agreement whereby it retains some of its power while conceding its hold over the Seven Kingdoms to one of the other more powerful states.

Game of Thrones has not really been too concerned with diplomacy. We see signs of it in Season 7 when the alliance is forming. This, arguably, is because of the threat each state felt to its own survival and therefore the need they had to band together. Will diplomacy still work after the war with the White Walkers is over? It remains to be seen. A bond has formed between Daenerys and Jon Snow. He has conceded power to her, though Sansa Stark may have something to say about this when she finds out.

Thus, the chance for a diplomatic resolution between at least these two countries is probable. If Cersei sees no way of winning, she too may agree to some sort of negotiations, though this seems unlikely as Daenerys does not appear to want to take no for an answer when it comes to her ruling the Seven Kingdoms. Daenerys is especially unlikely to negotiate if she comes out of the war in a position of power. Cersei, too, will not want to negotiate with Daenerys or Jon Snow if her power remains intact. Because the North is more known for its value in the rule of law, out of the three, they are the most likely to engage in diplomatic relations with all parties, or at least attempt to avoid another war.

Season 8 unfolds in much the way we expected. The alliance suffers many casualties, but does, ultimately, defeat the White Walkers thanks to Arya's stealthy assassin skills. Though the alliance is victorious, Cersei is emboldened further that she can win a war against Daenerys given the large number of casualties suffered. Daenerys, too, though, seems even more sure of her ability to win the Iron Throne for herself after winning the war with the White Walkers. With no international body to force the states to cooperate, "The Last War" is inevitable as a result.

The finale of Season 8 sees Daenerys become consumed with her quest for power (perhaps fueled by her recent victory or grief at the loss she has suffered) and to annihilate King's Landing, killing not only Cersei but thousands of innocent people. Fans were surprised (and disappointed) by this seeming turn of events (Guillaume 2019). Lord Acton, a British historian, likely would not have been, though. "Power tends to corrupt, and absolute power corrupts absolutely," he once famously said. Of course, it might not be as simple as this. Daenerys suffered great loss not just from the Great War, but when Missandei is beheaded by Cersei. She also loses a second of her three dragons—whom she considers her children (*Game of Thrones*, Season 8, Episode 5). Her actions could have been a result of the environment in which she faced and the harsh realities she has had to deal with and not just because the power "went to her head." There was also no other means by which Cersei's claim to the throne could be challenged, leaving the reliance on compliance with international law not an option since none exists at this time.

The series closes with a meeting of the victors of the war discussing how to divvy up power. Samwell Tarley suggests it should be up to the people to select their ruler. "Why just us [decide who rules]," he asks? "We represent all the great houses, but whoever we choose won't just rule over lords and ladies. Maybe who we choose should be chosen by everyone" (*Game of Thrones*, Season 8, Episode 6). This statement represents a definitive departure from power politics and one toward democratic representation of the people. Of course, Sam's suggestion is met with laughter from the others. It is not surprising, though, since those in power have shown it is difficult to give it up completely.

A compromise between Samwell Tarly's recommendation and what existed before—a ruler chosen because of birth—is struck. The ruler of the Six Kingdoms (since the North declares its independence) would be chosen instead of inheriting the throne, but he or she would be selected by those in power, of course, and not by the general populous. Thus, Bran Stark is voted into power by the nobles. Though, still not a democracy as we think of one, it is the first signs of democratic institutions being established. Importantly, it is being done in an effort to make certain future wars because of power politics do not occur.

Many fans, reportedly, were not happy with this ending, thinking "Bran was an unlikely candidate to end up on the throne as it seemed like his role as the Three-Eyed Raven would keep him busy enough," (McCluskey 2019, para. 15). However, in the last scene we see the king's council convene. Bran comes in, but only stays briefly, leaving his council to work out the specifics of any business to be addressed. The council, though, exhibits signs of democratic characteristics with each member expressing different viewpoints on what to do with matters relating to the budget and military. Thus, Bran's opinion on how to proceed does not dominate the conversation, leaving others free to express their own thoughts. This type of approach to decision-making produces better policy results (Allison 1969). It is also more indicative of a democratic system, especially compared to the authoritarian rule of Robert, Joffrey, Cersei, and even Daenerys—for even though they had councils similar to Bran's, at the end of the day, it was what they wanted that mattered most.

The new power arrangement stems from the fact no one wants to see another war. After WWI, and especially WWII, the world, too, began to restructure itself in a way to help promote cooperation. International organizations, like the League of Nations and, later, the United Nations, were established as forums for states to work out their differences in a manner consistent with established international norms and laws. Though conflict still occurs, large scale wars are far fewer than in the past.

International relations is a dynamic field that encompasses several different paradigms, all of which seek to explain why states behave the way they do. Its ability to explain behavior in the real world as well as in a series like *Game of Thrones* shows its flexibility. Though it may not be possible to always accurately predict how states will behave (e.g., Jon Snow stabbing Daenerys), in such a complex world these theories help simplify things in a way that makes it much easier to understand.

Bibliography

Adler, Emanuel and Michael N. Barnett. 1998. *Security Communities*. Cambridge: Cambridge University Press.

Alfred, Gerald R. and Franke Wilmer. 1997. "Indigenous Peoples, States and Conflict." In *Wars in the Midst of Peace*, eds. David Carment and Patrick James. Pittsburgh: University of Pittsburgh Press, 26–44.

Allison, Graham. 1969. "Conceptual Models and the Cuban Missile Crisis." *American Political Science Review* 63: 689–718.

Amnesty International. 2017. *Amnesty International Report 2016/17: The State of the World's Human Rights*. London: Amnesty International Ltd.

Arat, Zehra F. Kabasakal. 2006. *Human Rights Worldwide: A Reference Handbook*. Santa Barbara: ABC-CLIO, Inc.

Ashcroft, Bill, Gareth Griffiths, and Helen Tiffin. 2000. *Post-Colonial Studies: The Key Concepts*. London: Routledge.

Barua, 1996. "Television, Politics, and the Epic Heroine: Case Study, Sita." In *Between The Lines: South Asians and Postcoloniality*, eds. Deepika Bahri and Mary Vasudeva. Philadelphia: Temple University Press, 216–236.

Beier, J. Marshall. 2005. *International Relations in Uncommon Places: Indigeneity, Cosmology, and the Limits of International Theory*. New York: Palgrave Macmillan.

Block, Sharon. 2006. *Rape and Sexual Power in Early America*. Chapel Hill: University of North Carolina Press.

Boswell, Terry and C. Chase-Dunn. 2000. *The Spiral of Capitalism and Socialism*. Boulder, CO: Rienner.

Bruyneel, Kevin. 2007. *The Third Space of Sovereignty: The Postcolonial Politics of U.S.-Indigenous Relations*. Minneapolis: University of Minnesota Press.

Byrd, Jodi A. and Michael Rothberg. 2011. "Between Subalternity and Indigeneity." *Interventions* 13 (1): 1–12.

Brysk, Alison and Arturo Jimenez. 2012. "The Globalization of Law: Implications for the Fulfillment of Human Rights." *Journal of Human Rights* 11: 4–16.

Bueno de Mesquita, Bruce, Alastair Smith, Randolph Siverson, and James Morrow. 2004. *The Logic of Political Survival*. Cambridge: MIT Press.

Cavalcanti, Tiago V., Stephen L. Parente, and Rui Zhao. 2007. "Religion in Macroeconomics: A Quantitative Analysis of Weber's Thesis." *Economic Theory* 32: 105–123.

CBC. 2007. "Canada Votes 'No' as UN Native Rights Declared." *CBC*, September 13. https://www.cbc.ca/news/canada/canada-votes-no-as-un-native-rights-declaration-passes-1.632160.

Clark, Ann Marie. 2001. *Diplomacy of Conscience*. Princeton: Princeton University Press.

Coletta, Amanda. 2018. "Third World Conditions: Many of Canada's Indigenous People Can't Drink the Water at Home." *The Washington Post*, October 15. https://www.washingtonpost.com/world/the_americas/third-world-conditions-many-of-canadas-indigenous-people-cant-drink-the-water-at-home/2018/10/14/c4f429b4-bc53-11e8-8243-f3ae9c99658a_story.html?noredirect=on.

Collins, A. 1995. *The Security Dilemma and the End of the Cold War*. New York: Keele University Press.

Columbus, Christopher. 1893. *The Journal of Christopher Columbus (During His First Voyage 1492–1493)*. Translated by Clements R. Markham, C. B., F.R.S. London: Hakluyt Society.

Connelly, Matthew. 2003. *A Diplomatic Revolution: Algeria's Fight for Independence and the Origins of the Post-Cold War Era.* Oxford: Oxford University Press.

Connor, Walker. 1978. "A Nation Is a Nation, Is a State, Is an Ethnic Group Is a . . . " *Ethnic and Racial Studies* 1 (4): 377–400.

Cooper, Frederick. 2005. *Colonialism in Question: Theory, Knowledge, History.* Berkeley: University of California Press.

Donnelly, Jack. 2013. *Universal Human Rights in Theory and Practice.* Ithaca: Cornell University Press

Dorff, Robert "Robin" H., 2004. "Some Basic Concepts and Approaches in the Study of International Relations." In *U.S. Army War College Guide to National Security Policy and Strategy,* ed. J. Boone Bartholomees. Pennsylvania: Diane Publishing.

Dorris, Michael. 1987. "Indians on the Shelf." In *The American Indian and the Problem of History,* ed. Calvin Martin. New York: Oxford University Press, 233–247.

Doyle, Michael. 1997. *Ways of War and Peace.* New York: W.W. Norton Company.

Doyle, Michael. 1986. "Liberalism and World Politics," *American Political Science Review* 80: 1151–70.

Dusza, Karl. 1989. "Max Weber's Conception of the State." *International Journal of Politics, Culture, and Society* 3(1) (Autumn), 71–105.

Evans, Graham and Jeffrey Newnham. 1998. *The Penguin Dictionary of International Relations.* New York: Penguin Books.

Flood, Alison. 2018. "George RR Martin: 'When I Began a *Game of Thrones* I Thought It Would Be a Short Story." *The Guardian.* Retrieved from https://www.theguardian.com/books/2018/nov/10/books-interview-george-rr-martin

Fukuyama, Francis. 2011. *The Origins of Political Order: From Pre-Human Times to the French Revolution.* New York: Farrar, Straus and Girous.

Game of Thrones, "The Broken Man." Season 6, Episode 7. Directed by Mark Mylod. Written by Bryan Cogman. Home Box Office, Inc. June 5, 2016.

Game of Thrones, "And Now His Watch Is Ended." Season 3, Episode 4. Directed by Alex Graves. Written by David Benioff and D. B. Weiss. Home Box Office, Inc. April 21, 2013.

Game of Thrones. "Fire and Blood." Season 1, Episode 10. Directed by Alan Taylor. Written by David Benioff and D. B. Weiss. Home Box Office, Inc. June 19, 2011.

Game of Thrones. "The North Remembers." Season 2, Episode 1. Directed by Alan Taylor. Written by David Benioff and D. B. Weiss. Home Box Office, Inc. April 12, 2012.

Game of Thrones. "The Lion and the Rose." Season 4, Episode 2. Directed by Alex Graves. Written by David Benioff and D. B. Weiss. Home Box Office, Inc. April 13, 2014.

Game of Thrones. "The Mountain and the Viper." Season 4, Episode 8. Directed by Alex Graves. Written by David Benioff and D. B. Weiss. Home Box Office, Inc. June 1, 2014.

Game of Thrones. "The Watchers on the Wall." Season 4, Episode 9. Directed by Neil Marshall. Written by David Benioff and D. B. Weiss. Home Box Office, Inc. June 8, 2014.

Game of Thrones, "The House of Black and White." Season 5, Episode 2. Directed by Michael Slovis. Written by David Benioff and D. B. Weiss. Home Box Office, Inc. April 19, 2015.

Game of Thrones, "The Iron Throne." Season 8, Episode 6. Directed by David Benioff and D. B. Weiss. Written by David Benioff and D. B. Weiss. Home Box Office, Inc. May 19, 2019.

Game of Thrones "Oathkeeper." Season 4, Episode 4. Directed by Michelle MacLaren. Written by Bryan Cogman. *Home Box Office,* April 27, 2014.

Game of Thrones, "The Old Gods and the New." Season 2, Episode 6. Directed by David Nutter. Written by Vanessa Taylor. Home Box Office. May 6, 2012.

Game of Thrones, "Cripples, Bastards, and Broken Things." Season 1, Episode 4. Directed by Brian Kirk. Written by Bryan Cogman. Home Box Office, May 8, 2011.

Game of Thrones, "You Win or You Die." Season 1, Episode 7. Directed by Daniel Minahan. Written by David Benioff and D. B. Weiss. Home Box Office. May 29, 2011.

Game of Thrones, "The North Remembers," Season 2, Episode 1. Directed by Alan Taylor. Written by David Benioff and D. B. Weiss. Home Box Office. April 8, 2012.

Game of Thrones, "A Man without Honor," Season 2, Episode 7. Directed by David Nutter. Written by David Benioff and D. B. Weiss. Home Box Office. May 13, 2012.

Game of Thrones, "The Prince of Winterfell," Season 2, Episode 8. Directed by Alan Taylor. Written by David Benioff and D. W. Weiss. Home Box Office. May 20, 2012.

Game of Thrones, "The Wars to Come." Season 5, Episode 1. Directed by Michael Slovis. Written by David Benioff and D. W. Weiss. Home Box Office. April 12, 2015.

Game of Thrones, "The House of Black and White." Season 5, Episode 2. Directed by Michael Slovis. Written by David Benioff and D. B. Weiss. Home Box Office. April 19, 2015.

Game of Thrones. "Dragonstone." Season 7, Episode 1. Directed by Jeremy Podeswa. Written by David Benioff and D. B. Weiss. July 16, 2017.

Game of Thrones. "The Spoils of War." Season 7, Episode 4. Directed by Matt Shakman. Written by David Benioff and D. B. Weiss. August 6, 2017.

Game of Thrones. "Beyond the Wall." Season 7, Episode 6. Directed by Alan Taylor. Written by David Benioff and D. B. Weiss. August 20, 2017.

Game of Thrones. "The Bells." Season 8, Episode 5. Directed by Alan Taylor. Written by David Benioff and D. B. Weiss. May 12, 2019.

Gartzke, Erik. 2007. "The Capitalist Peace." *American Journal of Political Science* 51 (1): 166–191.

Graubart, Karen B. 2007. *With Our Labor and Sweat: Indigenous Women and the Formation of Colonial Society in Peru 1550–1700*. Stanford: Stanford University Press.

Greico, Richard. 1988. "Anarchy and the Limits of Cooperation: A Realist Critique of the Newest Liberal Institutionalism." *International Organization* 42(3) (Summer): 485–507.

Guillaume, Jenna. (2019, May 19). "The *Game of Thrones* Finale Was a Mess and People Are Disappointed." *BuzzFeed*. Retrieved from https://www.buzzfeed.com/jennaguillaume/game-of-thrones-season-8-finale-fan-reactions

Gurr, Ted Robert. 2000. *People versus States: Minorities at Risk in the New Century*. Washington, DC: United States Institute of Peace Press.

Harris, Nathaniel. 2009. *Systems of Governmennt Monarchy*. Evans Brothers.

Hasenclever, Andreas, Peter Mayer, and Volker Rittberger. 1996. "Interest, Power, Knowledge: The Study of International Regimes." *Mershon International Studies Review* 40(2), (October 1).

Hughes, Sarah. 2014. "'Sopranos Meets Middle-Earth': How *Game of Thrones* Took over Our World." (March 22). Retrieved from https://www.theguardian.com/tv-and-radio/2014/mar/22/game-of-thrones-whats-not-to-love.

ILO. 2017. "Indigenous and Tribal Peoples Convention, 1989 (No. 169)." *ILO*. http://www.ilo.org/dyn/normlex/en/f?p=NORMLEXPUB:12100:0::NO::P12100I LO_CODE:C169.

Indian Law. 2017. "American Declaration on the Rights of Indigenous Peoples." *Indian Law*. http://indianlaw.org/sites/default/files/ADRIP%201-17-17.pdf.

Kant, Immanuel. 1887. *The Philosophy of Law*, trans. W. Hastie. Edinburgh: T. and T. Clark.

Katzenstein, Peter. 1996. *The Culture of National Security: Norms and Identity in World Politics*. New York: Columbia University Press.

Katzenstein, Peter J. 1996. "Introduction: Alternative Perspectives on National Security." In *The Culture of National Security*, ed. Peter Katzenstein. New York: Columbia University Press, 1–33.

Keohane, Robert O. 1989. *After Hegemony: Cooperation and Discord in the World Political Economy*. New York: Princeton University Press.

Keohane, Robert and Joseph Nye. 2001. *Power and Interdependence*, 3rd ed. New York: Addison Wesley Longman.

Kooijmans, P. 1986. "Torture and Other Cruel, Inhuman or Degrading Treatment or Punishment: Report by the Special Rapporteur, Mr. P. Kooijmans, Appointed Pursuant to Commission on Human Rights Resolution 1985/33." *UN ECOSOC.* http://undocs.org/E/CN.4/1986/15.

Krasner, Stephen D. 2009. *Power, the State, and Sovereignty: Essays on International Relations.* New York: Routledge.

Kumar, Krishan. 2010. "Nation-States as Empires, Empires as Nation-States: Two Principles One Practice?" *Springer Science+Business Media.* (January).

La Tercera. 2017. "La crítica de género de Bachelet: Las mujeres lideres son evaluadas por como lucen." *La Tercera,* September 22. https://www.latercera.com/noticia/la-critica-genero-bachelet-las-mujeres-lideres-evaluadas-lucen/

Laskowski, Amy. 2017. "The Languages of *Game of Thrones*: CAS Linguist on the Origins of Dothraki, Valyrian." *Boston University Today,* July 12. http://www.bu.edu/today/2017/game-of-thrones-languages/.

Lightfoot, Sheryl. 2016. *Global Indigenous Politics: A Subtle Revolution.* New York: Routledge.

Lindroth, Marjo and Heidi Sinevaara-Niskanen. 2018. *Global Politics and Its Violent Care for Indigeneity: Sequels to Colonialism.* New York: Palgrave Macmillan.

Lopes, Cátia and Noëlle Quénivet. 2008. "Individuals as Subjects of International Humanitarian Law and Human Rights Law." In *International Humanitarian Law and Human Rights Law: Towards a New Merger in International Law,* eds. Roberta Arnold and Noëlle Quénivet. Leiden: Koninklijke Brill, NV, 199–236.

Macklem, Patrick. 2015. "Human Rights in International Law: Three Generations or One?" *London Review of International Law* 3 (1): 61–92.

Marx, Karl and Friedrich Engles. 2008. *On Religion.* New York: Dover Publications, Inc.

McCluskey, Megan. (2019, May 20). "Here's Who Ended Up on the Throne in the *Game of Thrones* Season Finale." *Time.* Retrieved from https://time.com/5591578/game-of-thrones-ending-winner/

McDonald, Brad. 2018. "International Trade: Commerce among Nations." IMF.org. Retrieved from https://www.imf.org/external/pubs/ft/fandd/basics/trade.htm.

Mearsheimer, John. 2001. *The Tragedy of Great Power Politics.* New York: W.W. Norton.

———. 1994. "The False Promise of International Institutions." *International Security* 19(3) (Winter): 5–49.

Metro-Goldwyn-Mayer Pictures presents a Marc Platt production; produced by Marc Platt, Ric Kidney; screenplay by Karen McCullah Lutz and Kirsten Smith; directed by Robert Luketic. Legally Blonde. [Santa Monica, CA]: MGM Home Entertainment, 2006.

Morgenthau, Hans J. 1978. *Politics among Nations: The Struggle for War and Peace,* 5th Edition. New York: Alfred A. Knopf.

Morgenthau, Hans. 1948. *Politics among Nations: The Struggle for Power and Peace.* New York: Alfred A. Knopf.

Nickel, James W. 1987. *Making Sense of Human Rights: Philosophical Reflections on the Universal Declaration of Human Rights.* Los Angeles: University of California Press.

Niezen, Ronald. 2003. *The Origins of Indigenism: Human Rights and the Politics of Identity.* Berkeley: University of California Press.

Nye, Joseph S. Jr. 2009. *Soft Power: The Means to Success in World Politics.* New York: Public Affairs.

OHCHR. 2017. "Torture Is Torture, and Waterboarding Is Not an Exception—UN Expert Urges the US Not to Reinstate It." *OHCHR.* https://www.ohchr.org/en/NewsEvents/Pages/DisplayNews.aspx?NewsID=21129&LangID=E.

OHCHR. 2013. "Free, Prior and Informed Consent of Indigenous Peoples." *United Nations Office of the Commissioner on Human Rights,* September. https://www.ohchr.org/Documents/Issues/ipeoples/freepriorandinformedconsent.pdf.

OHCHR. 2011. "Interpretation of Torture in Light of the Practice and Jurisprudence of International Bodies." *OHCHR*. https://www.ohchr.org/Documents/Issues/Torture/UNVFVT/Interpretation_torture_2011_EN.pdf.

OHCHR. 2008. "Promotion and Protection of All Human Rights, Civil, Political, Economic, Social, and Cultural Rights, Including the Right to Development." *OHCHR*. https://documents-dds-ny.un.org/doc/UNDOC/GEN/G08/101/61/PDF/G0810161.pdf?OpenElement.

OHCHR. 1990. "Convention on the Rights of the Child." *OHCHR*. https://www.ohchr.org/en/professionalinterest/pages/crc.aspx.

OHCHR. 1987. "Convention Against Torture." *OHCHR*. https://www.ohchr.org/en/professionalinterest/pages/cat.aspx.

OHCHR. 1966. "International Covenant on Economic, Social and Cultural Rights." *OHCHR*. https://www.ohchr.org/en/professionalinterest/pages/cescr.aspx.

OHCHR. 1966. "International Covenant on Civil and Political Rights." *OHCHR*. https://www.ohchr.org/en/professionalinterest/pages/ccpr.aspx.

Otterson, Joe. 2017. "*Game of Thrones* Season 7 Shatters *HBO* Ratings Records." *Variety*. (July 17). Retrieved from http://variety.com/2017/tv/news/game-of-thrones-season-7-premiere-ratings-1202497751/

Overy, Richard. 2003. "The Nuremberg Trials: International Law in the Making." In *From Nuremburg to The Hague: The Future of International Criminal Justice*, ed. Philippe Sands. Cambridge: Cambridge University Press, 1–30.

Oye, Kenneth A. 1986. "Explaining Cooperation under Anarchy." In *Cooperation under Anarchy*, ed., Kenneth A. Oye. Princeton: Princeton University Press, 1–24.

Pallotta, Frank. 2019. "*Game of Thrones* Finale Set New Viewship Record." *CNNBusiness.com* (May 20). Retrieved from https://www.cnn.com/2019/05/20/media/game-of-thrones-finale-ratings/index.html

Parenti, Michael. 2006. *The Culture Struggle*. Toronto, Ontario: Seven Stories Press.

Pilbeam, David R. 1970. *The Evolution of Man*. New York: Funk and Wagnalls.

Roberson, Joe. (2016, Aug. 10). "Who Has the Biggest Army on *Game of Thrones*?" *Zimbio*. Retrieved from http://www.zimbio.com/Beyond+the+Tube/articles/EjqjJTiNLgf/Biggest+Army+Game+Thrones

Rosato, Sebastian. 2003. "The Flawed Logic of the Democratic Peace." *American Political Science Review* 97 (4) (Nov.): 585–602.

Rosecrance, Richard. 1986. *The Rise of the Trading State: Commerce and Coalitions in the Modern World*. New York: Basic Books.

Roseau, James N. 2018. *Thinking Theory Thoroughly: Coherent Approaches to an Incoherent World*. New York: Routledge.

Rosenau, James N. and Mary Durfee. 1995. *Thinking Theory Through: Coherent Approaches to an Incoherent World*. Boulder: Westview Press.

Rothgeb, John M. 1993. *Defining Power: Influence and Force in the Contemporary International System*. New York: St. Martin's Press.

Rousseau, Jean-Jacques. 1762. "On the Social Contract; or, Principles of Political Rights." France.

Russett, Bruce. 1993. *Grasping the Democratic Peace*. Princeton University Press.

Sarason, Irwin G. and Barbara R. Sarason. 2009. "Social Support: Mapping the Construct." *Journal of Social and Personal Relationships* 26(1), DOI: 10.1177/0265407509105526.

Satran, Joe and Tiara Chiaramonte. 2017. "This Map of Westeros Shows the European Equivalents of the Seven Kingdoms." *Huffington Post*. Retrieved from https://www.huffingtonpost.com/2015/06/19/westeros-europe_n_7565694.html

Schrover, M. 2008. "Migration Policy and Media-hypes, the Netherlands 1945–2000." *European Social Science and History Conference. Lisbon*. Vol. 26.

Shannon, Vaughn P. 2000. "Norms Are What States Make of Them: The Political Psychology of Norm Violation." *International Studies Quarterly* 44: 293–316.

Shelton, Diana. 2000. "Introduction: Law, Non-Law and the Problem of 'Soft Law.'" In *Commitment and Compliance: The Role of Non-Binding Norms in the International Legal System*, ed. Diana Shelton. New York: Oxford University Press, 1–20.

———. 2000. "Commentary and Conclusion." In *Commitment and Compliance: The Role of Non-Binding Norms in the International Legal System*, ed. Diana Shelton. New York: Oxford University Press, 449–464.

Simmons, Beth. 2009. *Mobilizing for Human Rights: International Law in Domestic Politics.* New York: Cambridge University Press.

Singer, David J. 1961. "The Level-of-Analysis Problem in International Relations." *World Politics* 14 (1): 77–92.

Spivak, Gayatri Chakravorty. 1999. *Critique of Post-Colonial Reason: Toward a History of the Vanishing Present.* Cambridge: Harvard University Press.

Stein, Arthur A. 1982. "Coordination and Collaboration: Regimes in an Anarchic World." *International Organization* 36: 299–324.

Stroessinger, John G. 2010. *Why Nations Go to War.* 11th edition. Boston: Wadsworth Cengage Learning.

Tatum, Beverly Daniel. 1999. *"Why Are All the Black Kids Sitting Together in the Cafeteria?" and Other Conversations about Race.* New York: Basic Books.

Tickner, Ann. 2001. *Gendering World Politics.* New York: Columbia University Press.

Tilly, Charles. 1992. *Coercion, Capital, and European States, AD 990–1992.* Cambridge and Oxford: Blackwell.

———. 1975. *The Formation of National States in Western Europe.* Princeton: Princeton University Press.

UN. 2007. "61/295. United Nations Declaration on the Rights of Indigenous Peoples." *United Nations General Assembly*, October 2. https://documents-dds-ny.un.org/doc/UNDOC/GEN/N06/512/07/PDF/N0651207.pdf?OpenElement.

UN Committee. 1992. "CEDAW General Recommendation No. 19: Violence Against Women." *UN Committee on the Elimination of Discrimination Against Women (CEDAW).* http://www.refworld.org/docid/52d920c54.html.

UN Women. 2018. "Convention on the Elimination of All Forms of Discrimination Against Women." *UN Women.* http://www.un.org/womenwatch/daw/cedaw/text/econvention.htm.

United Nations. 2018a. "Charter of the United Nations." *UN.* http://www.un.org/en/charter-united-nations/.

United Nations. 2018b. "Universal Declaration of Human Rights." *UN.* http://www.un.org/en/universal-declaration-human-rights/.

Vasak, K. "Pour une troisième génération des droit de l'homme." In *Studies and Essays on International Humanitarian Law and Red Cross Principles in Honour of Jean Pictet*, ed. C. Swinarski. The Hague: Martinus Nijhoff, 837–850.

Wallerstein, Immanuel, 1974. *The Modern World-System: Capitalist Agriculture and the Origins of the European World-Economy in the Sixteenth Century.* New York: Academic Press.

Walt, Stephen M. 2013. "Which Works Best: Force or Diplomacy?" *Foreign Policy.* (August 21). Retrieved from https://foreignpolicy.com/2013/08/21/which-works-best-force-or-diplomacy/

Waltz, Kenneth. 1979. *Theory of International Politics.* New York: McGraw Hill.

———. 1988. "The Origins of Neorealist Theory." *The Journal of Interdisciplinary History* 18 (4): 615–628.

———. 1986. "Reductionist and Systemic Theories." *NeoRealism and Its Critics*, eds. Robert Keohane. New York: Columbia University Press.

———. 1959. *Man, The State, and War: A Theoretical Analysis.* New York: Columbia University Press.

Weber, Max. 1958. "Politics as Vocation." In *From Max Weber: Essays in Sociology*, eds. H. H. Gerth and C. W. Mills. New York: Oxford University Press, 77–128.

Weissbrodt, David and Isabel Hörtreiter. 1999. "The Principle of Non-Refoulement: Article 3 of the Convention Against Torture and Other Cruel, Inhuman or Degrading Treatment or Punishment in Comparison with the Non-Refoulement Provisions of Other International Human Rights Treaties." *Buffalo Human Rights Law Review* 5 (1): 1–73.

Wilmer, Franke. 1993. *The Indigenous Voice in World Politics.* Thousand Oaks: Sage Publications, Inc.

Wendt, Alexander. 1999. *Social Theory of International Politics.* Cambridge: Cambridge University Press.

Wenke, Robert J. 1999. *Patterns In Pre-History.* 4th ed. New York: Oxford University Press.

World Happiness Report. 2018.

Young, Laura D. 2013. "The Evolution of the Modern State." PhD diss, *Purdue University*, West Lafayette, Indiana. Department of Political Science.

Young, Laura D., Ñusta Carranza Ko, and Michael Perrin, 2018. "Using *Game of Thrones* to Teach International Relations," *Journal of Political Science Education.* DOI: 10.1080/15512169.2017.1409

Index

The Hound, 24
Hobbes, Thomas, 23

idealism. *See* Theories of International Relations
ideas, 55, 58, 60, 61, 68, 72
image I. *See* Theories of International Relations
image II. *See* Theories of International Relations
image III. *See* Theories of International Relations
Indigenous rights, 91
individual level. *See* levels of analysis
institutions, 7, 8, 14n2, 19, 37, 39, 40, 46, 48–50, 52, 55, 57, 60, 61, 63, 70, 72, 72n1, 91, 97, 105
International Covenant on Civil and Political Rights in 1966 (ICCPR), 76, 77
International Covenant on Economic, Social, and Cultural Rights (ICESCR), 77
International Labor Organization (ILO) Convention 169, 92
International Relations: anarchy, relation to, 19; definition, 2, 7, 14n2; focus, 2, 3, 21; *Game of Thrones*, relation to, 3, 5; theories, 9, 15, 23, 25, 39, 55, 56, 68, 70, 72, 89, 91, 99, 105. *See also* Theories of International Relations

Kant, Immanuel, 49, 50
King's Landing, 5, 7, 11, 13, 15, 16, 17–18, 20, 21, 23–24, 25, 26, 27, 29, 31, 32, 33, 34, 36, 38, 40, 41, 43, 44, 49, 59, 63, 83, 95, 102, 103, 104

Lannister, House of
Lannister, Cersei, 1, 3, 4, 16, 17, 18, 20, 23, 24, 25, 26, 29, 31, 41, 83, 95, 96, 102–103, 103–104, 105
Lannister, Jamie, 15, 17, 69
Lannister, Tyrion, 16, 45, 57, 61, 70, 81, 86
latent power. *See* power; latent power
level of analysis, 15, 15–16, 17, 18, 19, 20; individual, 15, 16, 24, 42, 55, 57;

domestic/state, 17, 18, 43, 45, 73, 92; system/international, 7, 19, 20, 65, 66; liberalism. *See* Theories of International Relations

Machiavelli, 23
Marxism. *See* Theories of International Relations
middle power. *See* power; middle power
military power. *See* power; military power
multipolar system, 24, 36

neo-liberalism. *See* Theories of International Relations
neo-realism. *See* Theories of International Relations
norms: levels of analysis, 18, 19; liberalism, 39, 48–49, 50, 51, 52; constructivism, 55, 56, 57, 58, 60–62, 63, 66, 70; human rights, 75, 78, 80, 84, 87; Indigenous peoples, 89, 92
The North, 1, 4, 6, 7, 8, 9, 10, 11, 13, 15, 16, 17–18, 20, 21, 24, 25, 26, 28, 31, 33, 34, 36, 38, 40, 41, 43, 47, 59, 61, 63, 70, 97, 101, 102, 103, 105

offensive realism. *See* offensive realist
offensive realist, 35, 36
optimism, 25, 55
optimal solution. *See* Prisoner's Dilemma

parity, 30
pessimism, 25
political realism. *See* Theories of International Relations
power: absolute power, 29, 30, 57, 104; definition, 28; economic power, 30, 44; great power, 7, 31, 32, 32–33, 34, 35–36, 52, 56; hard power, 30; hegemon, 34, 35, 36, 38, 52, 69; latent power, 28–29; middle power, 31, 33; military power, 29, 31, 32, 46, 48; power maximization, 52; relative power, 28, 29, 30, 35; small power, 31, 33, 34; soft power, 30; superpower, 31, 33

About the Authors

Laura D. Young is assistant professor of political science at Georgia Gwinnett College. She received her PhD in political science from Purdue University with a concentration in international relations, comparative politics, and political behavior and institutions. Her research interests focus on security studies, specifically issues related to environmental crises and resource scarcity and the resulting impact of these events on state development.

Ñusta Carranza Ko is assistant professor of global affairs and human security in the School of Public and International Affairs at the University of Baltimore. She received her PhD in political science from Purdue University and holds master's and bachelor's degrees from New York University, University of Windsor, and McGill University. Her research interests include cross-regional research on human rights and transitional justice processes in Latin America and East Asia, including policies of memorialization in Peru and South Korea and questions of Indigenous peoples' rights, namely forced sterilization, and Indigenous identities in Peru.